Mis-3-meanours

Second Runner-Up

Sally-Ann Fawcett

To Jessica
sending lots of love!
Sally-Ann Fawcett xx

RB
Rossendale Books

Published by Lulu Enterprises Inc.
3101 Hillsborough Street
Suite 210
Raleigh, NC 27607-5436
United States of America

Published in paperback 2017
Category: Popular Culture
Copyright Sally-Ann Fawcett © 2017
ISBN 978-0-244-93680-8

Acknowledgements

When I first began writing *Misdemeanours: Beauty Queen Scandals* in 2013, I had no idea that it would lead to two further volumes.

But, like death and taxes, controversy within the pageant world is almost a given. The very nature of the glamorous, exciting and brave women (and men) who choose to take part means that the beauty queen scene is never dull, and that a fascinating story is always round the corner!

What struck me, though, while researching the stories of those involved is that, no matter how difficult or controversial their situation, most of them managed to fight their way out of their predicament to earn real respect among the public and their peers. By salvaging reputations and righting wrongs, the ladies within those pages demonstrated the real meaning of redemption.

While it was entertaining for me to write about the trials and tribulations of the 'beauty queens gone bad', it was incredibly inspiring and satisfying when their stories turned out to have happy endings or, at the very least, a more positive resolution.

It is therefore to the beauty queens who have graced the pages of *Misdemeanours, More Misdemeanours* and now *Mis-3-meanours* that I dedicate the third volume of my trilogy. Without you, there would be no headlines, no glamour, and certainly no misdemeanours for me to write about!

I would like to send my sincere appreciation to the following for their contributions towards Mis-3-meanours:

- ❖ Journalist and lecturer Dr Martha Evans for her insight into the decision to stage Miss World at Sun City, in her book *Broadcasting the End of Apartheid: Live Television and the Birth of the New South Africa.*

- ❖ My special friend Ann Sidney, Miss World 1964, for talking to me so openly and honestly about her experiences for an exclusive inclusion in this book.

- ❖ Another very valued friend, Jon Osborne, for sharing his fascinating experiences as a director at the Miss World organisation for both *More Misdemeanours* and *Mis-3-meanours*. I feel extremely blessed to have made contact with him on Facebook all those years ago, having first set eyes on him within the pages of the Miss World programme in 1975.

- ❖ Richard Wendt for his fabulous cover design – www.richardwendtdesign.co.uk

- ❖ My mum Diane, dad John, sister Sue, niece Joanna, nephew Dougie, and husband Anthony - and all the amazing people and friends I have met in the pageant world for your unfailing support, enthusiasm and friendship.

Contents

Zara Holland, Miss Great Britain 2015

"It was the biggest mistake of my life. It cost me everything."

There is a time in many a low-budget horror film when one of the characters, convinced that their plans are watertight and fail-safe, proclaims the immortal line, "What could possibly go wrong?" - just before something, inevitably, goes horribly wrong.

That time-honoured line can't have been far from the lips of the two directors of the Miss Great Britain pageant, when the crown was placed safely on the head of Zara Holland, a petite and personable blonde from Hull, in September 2015.

Kate Solomons-Freakley and Jemma Simmonds had, after all, weathered the storm of rescuing the Miss Great Britain brand from its former status as a bit of a joke within the pageant world.

From its humble beginnings as a Bathing Beauty Contest in Morecambe in 1945, to a prestigious and top-rated TV show in the 70s and 80s, the pageant had - when Lancaster Council chose to end its association in 1989 - lurched from owner to owner and from one lurid news story to another. Over two turbulent decades the pageant had become tabloid fodder, an event not to be taken seriously unless you were a Page Three girl or reality TV wannabe.

So when Kate and Jemma, principals of Modelzed PR (now The Kreative Group), took over the pageant in 2013, it felt as though calm, prestige and common sense had been restored once again. The two of them staged glamorous and stylish finals in Leicester, with some heavy weight judges and solid but undramatic media, and three worthy winners under their sparkly belts.

So what could possibly go wrong?

Two words: *Love Island*.

Zara Holland was no newcomer to the pageant circuit. In 2014, at the age of 19, she was crowned Miss Hull & District and finished 7th in the Miss England final, after which a fledgling acting career had seen her appear in episodes of both *Emmerdale* and *Coronation Street*.

If Zara had held ambitions to further her on-screen fame by winning a major pageant, she kept them well hidden from the judges at the final of Miss Great Britain 2015, talking only of the designer boutique she owned with her mum Cheryl - herself a former beauty queen and antiques dealer on *David Dickinson's Real Deal* show - and her heartfelt desire to win the crown.

Ironically, one of the judges that night was Danielle Lloyd, the model-turned-reality star who had, until that point, been the most publicly-sacked beauty queen of modern times. Danielle had been fired as Miss Great Britain 2004 due to allegations of a relationship with one of the judges, football star Teddy Sheringham, prior to the pageant and for posing for *Playboy* magazine. Some years later, Danielle accepted an apology from the then-owners of the contest and was reinstated as the official winner, but not before the media and press attention given to her sacking had seen her become a household name, appearing in *Celebrity Big Brother, The Weakest Link, Total Wipeout*, and *Come Dine With Me*, among others.

Nobody had an inkling - including the author, who was also a judge that night - that Danielle's pageant infamy was about to be eclipsed by the new winner.

Until the Miss Great Britain final, Zara had been a model beauty queen, organising her own charitable events to raise funds for worthy causes and enthusiastically posting photos from such occasions on her social media sites. Indeed, she won the Miss Charity award on stage for having raised the most money of all the 50 finalists, as well as the Miss Beach Beauty title for best in swimwear.

But as soon as she had been crowned, pageant-watchers noticed that her Facebook posts were becoming rather less about raising money for charity, and more about raising her own profile. In between switching on the Christmas lights in her home town of Hull, she was seen out at events and parties with minor stars from reality TV and soaps, and on the red carpet of film premieres including *Dad's Army*.

But what really set alarm bells ringing in the Miss Great Britain office was when, a few weeks into her reign, Zara posed in lingerie for a series of pictures, in a photo shoot she had arranged herself. She had also contacted Kate and Jemma insisting that they try and land her a coveted spot in the *Celebrity Big Brother* house. When they failed to do so - due to the producers having already signed up enough stars for the next series - Zara went against the terms of her Miss Great Britain contract and signed with a management agency, convinced they would have more success in boosting her, hitherto hidden, TV dreams.

Zara had, they admitted, been a fantastic Miss Great Britain thus far with an amazing work ethic, attending all the events they had arranged for her, but concern was growing that their new winner was not only continually ignoring their pleas for her to credit ModelZed when posting about her appearances on social media, but choosing inappropriately revealing outfits that were opening her up to online mockery and uncomplimentary remarks.

When Zara decided to audition for the TV show *Take Me Out*, and her new manager suggested splitting any commission for appearances, ModelZed were forced to draw up a new, updated contract for her to sign. This, they hoped, would close the loopholes she seemed so keen to exploit, and would attempt to put themselves firmly back in the driving seat of her reign.

When nothing came of her *Take Me Out* audition, or one for reality show *Ex On The Beach*, Zara jumped - quite literally - at the chance of appearing on a winter sports competition on Channel Four. *The Jump* was created in 2014, and tested the prowess of celebrities as they attempted to master various snow-based sports, including the giant slalom, bobsleigh and skeleton.

After several of the competing celebrities had had to withdraw due to injury, Zara was called upon to don her sallopettes and head out to Austria to join the cast on the slopes.

However, Zara's reality show dreams took yet another battering when she was sent packing from the show before she had ever had a chance to appear on an episode. The producers feared her skills weren't up to scratch and, not wanting to risk yet another casualty, sent the piste-off beauty queen home less than 48 hours after her arrival.

At this stage, nearly halfway through her reign and after so many knock backs, Zara was becomingly increasingly frustrated at her lack of TV exposure, so when the producers of *Love Island* came calling, she grabbed the opportunity with both hands.

Love Island, an ITV2 reality show, pairs single men and woman on a sun-soaked island for five weeks, and the 2015 series had been slammed in the media for airing sex scenes between contestants in a bid to save it from being a ratings disaster.

Despite the programme's dubious reputation, Zara was waved off that June morning with the albeit reluctant blessing of Kate and Jemma at ModelZed, although not without their gaining her reassurance that she would avoid any sexual activity or unseemly behaviour while on the show.

Zara wouldn't be the only beauty queen on the island: she was joined by Sophie Gradon, Miss Great Britain 2009, and Malin Andersson, former finalist in Miss England, Miss Sweden and Miss Great Britain. But Zara was the only reigning beauty queen on the show, and as a result had far more at stake in terms of reputation.

Things didn't start well. Even before Zara had arrived on the show, an ex-boyfriend called Max Morley – who happened to have won the 2015 edition of *Love Island* – branded her 'boring' and 'prim and proper' in an interview with the *Daily Star*, stating that there 'wasn't a chance' that Zara would have sex while on the show.

Indeed, the first two weeks in the contestants' villa in Mallorca were, for main part, fairly dull and uneventful for Zara. Her habit of constantly reminding her companions that she was the reigning Miss Great Britain caused her to come in for some gentle ribbing on Twitter, but nothing in her behaviour gave any cause for worry or concern, even when she was consistently passed up by the men of the house for a female they preferred. If anything, she had the viewers' sympathy for the fact that she was the only girl who hadn't managed to couple up with a male contestant yet, when all those around her were sleeping together in the huge shared bedroom.

All that was about to change, in the most public and unexpected of ways. A 24 year old scaffolder by the name of Alex Bowen arrived on the island along with personal trainer James Khan, and the public voted for Zara to choose to have a date with either of them. Zara chose Alex, despite the fact that he had immediately set his sights on another islander, Olivia Buckland.

"I want to get to know Alex more," Zara said to the Beach Hut camera. "Why not? He's the new boy."

In his pre-entrance interview, Alex hadn't been overly enthusiastic at the prospect of meeting Zara. He found her 'a bit annoying' to watch on the show.

The twosome retired to the Hideaway to spend some time alone and to make full use of the champagne and strawberries provided. Zara explained to him why she had chosen Alex over James. "You caught my eye, so why not? It's your first night, so why not make it a night to remember?"

When Zara received a text from the production team asking if they wanted to stay in the Hideaway for the whole night or return to the villa, their decision - to stay - ensured it became a night that *everyone* would remember. In scenes set to the rousing climactic orchestration of *Land of Hope & Glory*, and edited carefully to show enough so as not to leave viewers in any doubt what was going on - including a lurid close-up of Zara licking her lips as she cuddled up to Alex - the couple had full sex within hours of first meeting each other.

The next morning, back in the villa, she faced disbelief from her fellow islanders that she had slept with Alex.

Fellow housemate Kady was incredulous at her friend's tryst. "Did you sleep with him? You slept with him! Zara, are you joking?" she gasped. "Zara, you shouldn't have slept with him!"

"What a stupid girl," Kady raged to the other islanders. "Why would she do that? Who's she going to cry to when he doesn't want to be with her? I'm so annoyed with her."

An anxious and downcast Zara disappeared into the Beach Hut to express her regrets about what had happened. "You know when you're in the moment and it just happens? That's really not like me at all. Why couldn't we have just gone to sleep?"

When, predictably, Alex immediately returned to wooing his original crush Olivia Buckland, a tearful Zara turned to the Beach Hut camera again to castigate herself further. "I'm really disappointed," she said. "It's my own fault, though. I can't blame anyone else for my own actions."

Seemingly aware that her Miss Great Britain crown may be in jeopardy, she confided in Sophie Gradon that she was worried about repercussions. Sophie, who won Miss Great Britain in 2009 and acrimoniously parted company with the-then owners before her reign was over, asked her if she'd be bothered if she were sacked.

"Yes, I would," Zara replied, honestly.

Meanwhile, the Twittersphere went into meltdown at the sight of the unexpected coupling between Zara and Alex, and over at Miss GB HQ, the phone was ringing off the hook. Kate and Jemma had been forewarned of their titleholder's actions between the sheets 24 hours earlier by *The Sun*, giving them time to collect their thoughts, make a decision and - more importantly - warn Zara's mum Cheryl of what she would be witnessing on screen that evening.

Their initial reaction was disappointment that Zara had reneged on her word to them, feelings shared by Cheryl, who initially had refused to believe what Kate had phoned to tell her. However, they held off making a firm decision until they had seen the footage themselves, issuing a statement to *The Sun* to say that while the organisation did not condone Zara's behaviour, they accepted that she was a 20-year-old woman whose actions were not controlled by them.

However, after the steamy scenes had been aired to a stunned nation, ModelZed were left with no choice but to take the ultimate step and, that same night, announced that Zara had been stripped of her title.

"Following recent actions within the ITV show *Love Island*," their statement said, "it is with deep regret that we, the Miss Great Britain organisation, have to announce that Zara Holland has been formally de-crowned as Miss Great Britain 2015/16."

The statement went on to say that despite being the oldest pageant in Britain, "we pride ourselves on promoting the positivity of pageants in modern society and this includes the promotion of a strong, positive female role model in our winners. We wholly accept that everyone make mistakes but Zara, as an ambassador for Miss Great Britain, simply did not uphold the responsibility expected of the title."

They would, they announced, be crowning first runner-up, Deone Robertson of North Lanarkshire, as the new Miss Great Britain for the remaining three months of the reign.

The next day, Zara was taken to one side and told off camera by production staff that she had been stripped of her Miss Great Britain title, at the same time giving her the option to leave if she wanted to.

A shell-shocked Zara went back outside to break the news. "I need to speak to everyone," she sobbed. "They've taken my title off me."

Zara chose to remain on the show, yet told the Beach Hut camera that she was "gutted." "I did Miss Great Britain because I wanted to," she said. "I put in the hard work and time and commitment and effort, and

I won. Now I made just one silly, stupid mistake of being in the moment and it's ruined everything."

Meanwhile her fellow islanders rallied round with support. This support, however, was nothing compared to that from the viewers, who bombarded social media in outrage that she had been sacked.

The show's host Caroline Flack tweeted, "Feel even more sorry for Zara now she's been de-crowned. What even is 'Miss GB'? Are we living in the dark ages?"

There were calls for Zara to be reinstated, slamming the Miss GB organisers for their 'small-minded', 'petty' and 'outdated' decisions, accusing them of bullying and shaming her. #MissGB and #Zara were trending on Twitter, while one fan organised an online petition calling for her to get her title back, which was signed by nearly 21,000 people in total.

The *Daily Telegraph* political correspondent Michael Wilkinson weighed in with an article which called them a 'disgrace' for priding themselves on being a platform for women's rights, yet shaming Zara by de-crowning her.

Some denounced the decision as sexist – "This public embarrassment wouldn't happen to a man" – while others pointed out that Zara was far more of a modern day role model than an outdated beauty queen spouting pleas for world peace.

Meanwhile, the two directors of ModelZed were being subjected to harassment on a grand and very distressing scale.

"It was absolutely horrendous," Director Kate Solomons-Freakley recalls. "I underestimated how many people would be so supportive of Zara and deem what she did as perfectly acceptable. I had never been so bullied - receiving emails and messages of hate, and phone calls at all hours.

"The night after Zara was de-crowned, the calls started at 10.30pm, so I switched my phone to silent, waking up at 2am to more missed calls and the most horrible voicemails. I could've justified every single thing we've done but I didn't have the time or the energy.

"People thought we were a big, corporate organisation with a firm to handle the PR, but it's just me and Jemma, two thirty-something married mums. We had spent the past four years working hard to turn the pageant around to change the lads' mags stereotypical image of Miss Great Britain, but Zara's actions undid it all.

"I was devastated, I really was."

News of Zara's de-crowning made headlines in every newspaper in the country, while websites all over the world reported the controversy, making her the most talked-about and infamous beauty queen of the internet age.

Two days after the sacking drama, Zara left *Love Island*. The ITV producers agreed that her mother should fabricate an illness in order to get Zara off the show, and she was seen announcing tearfully to her fellow islanders that she had to leave due to Cheryl's health.

Meanwhile, Cheryl herself told *The Sun* that although she was surprised by Zara's out of character behaviour and that it wasn't her "proudest moment", she didn't think her daughter had "committed any crime. I'm disappointed they took her title away. I was hoping they would understand that all young women make mistakes."

Jemma Simmonds, Events & Operations Director of Modelzed, defended their decision to release their statement immediately. "Of course we would've preferred to have told Zara face to face," she said, "but as we were allowed no contact with her while she was in the villa, this was taken out of our hands. She could potentially have been on the show for another three or four weeks; we couldn't leave that amount of time before making an announcement.

"It is not a prerequisite of the show that you have to have sex. We gave Zara permission to take part under the stipulation that she didn't have sex on TV. Zara fully agreed to this and knowingly went against our wishes."

Jemma also confirmed that she and Kate had left several voice messages for Zara as soon as she had returned to Britain, but that their calls hadn't been returned.

The new Miss Great Britain, Deone Robertson, who finished runner-up to Zara, told the *Mirror* that her inheritance of the crown was "bittersweet" under the circumstances, but understood why her predecessor had had to lose the crown.

"We are supposed to be role models for young girls and our chosen charities, and Zara knew this. Everyone is briefed before entering a pageant, there are contracts in place. You can't be seen naked or topless and definitely can't have sex on TV".

The British and international pageant community closed ranks and, in an unusual move in a highly competitive market, most directors of rival pageants posted on social media their agreement towards the decision by Kate and Jemma to de-crown their winner, suggesting they would follow suit under the same circumstances.

Upon her return home, Zara's new-found notoriety ensured she was hot property for magazine interviews and TV talk shows, and her first stop was an exclusive interview with *The Sun*, accompanied by a glossy photo shoot.

"I've done nothing wrong," she told the paper. "All women have needs."

Of the Miss Great Britain organisation, she claimed she hadn't heard from them since she left the show. "They gave me a written letter of permission to take part on *Love Island*, and they haven't spoken to me since. They didn't tell me I couldn't have sex on the show. It was horrific to lose the title."

Her one regret was letting her family down. "My mum seeing it on TV is the worst thing to ever happen. I was mortified, horrified. But it has happened now and I can only move forward."

And move forward she did – to Lorraine Kelly's morning show that same week, to talk further about how she felt returning to the UK into the eye of a media storm. Yet it was Lorraine herself who found herself the subject of the viewers' derision, accused on Twitter of being overly harsh towards her guest.

Zara explained how low in confidence she had been feeling on the show, and that her doubts about her looks and personality had been a factor towards her actions when locked in the Hideaway with the new boy. Viewers weren't impressed with Lorraine's 'judgemental' attitude in 'trying to make Zara feel bad'.

"What were you thinking?" Lorraine asked her. "Did you just forget that it was on the telly?"

When Zara repeated her claim that the Miss GB bosses hadn't told her not to have sex on national TV in their letter of permission to join *Love Island*, Lorraine replied, "They obviously thought, 'We don't need to put that in there'!"

"The way @reallorraine is talking to @zaraholland11 about Love Island is just perpetuating the idea that women should be ashamed of sex," said one tweet.

Another asked, "Why are women still shamed for making adult choices?"

It was generally considered at this stage, on social media at least, that Zara was still very much the victim who had been unfairly hung out to dry, and that the Miss GB people were the bad guys at fault.

Zara cited a migraine as to why she didn't join her fellow islanders at the glitzy wrap party following the conclusion of *Love Island*, but shortly afterwards was snapped by the paparazzi attending the beauty industry's White Party in London, and splashing in the sea during a holiday in Ibiza.

When Zara was invited onto the ITV daytime show *Loose Women* in August, many pageant-watchers expressed surprise that a fellow guest would be the woman who had inherited her crown, Deone Robertson. For some, it felt as though Kate and Jemma were re-opening old wounds in permitting the controversial debate to continue so publicly, yet it proved to be a masterstroke on their part.

Enough time had passed for the public's perception of Zara to shift from a sympathetic view to a more balanced one, and only a loyal few of those watching bothered to take to Twitter in outrage when the *Loose Women* panellists – including Andrea McLean, June Sarpong, Sherrie Hewson and Katie Price - showed her little mercy.

Zara faced the panel alone for the first part of the interview; Deone would come on stage later.

Sherrie asked, "Did you not consider for one second that you would lose that title, because you are supposed to be a role model for young girls out there?"

When Zara attempted to blame having drunk too much champagne, Sherrie interrupted. "That's not an excuse. Did you not think, I've just got that wonderful title, therefore I must hold myself back?"

June Sarpong weighed in by pointing out that the Miss Great Britain terms and conditions that Zara signed would've stated that the winner cannot bring the title into disrepute. "It's not that you had sex on TV," she continued, "but when you have a crown like that that has a kind of history and heritage – whether you agree with beauty pageants or not – if you behave like that you have to just to accept, fair enough, if they take it away from you."

"I disagree," replied Zara. "Miss Great Britain prides itself on being a modern day beauty pageant – we're living in 2016 now, we're not in the 1950s."

"Having sex on TV is not modern day," June interrupted.

"This is nothing to do with it being in 1950," Sherrie agreed. "It's to do with respect for you, yourself, your family."

"I don't agree with sex on TV either," Zara said, "but all I know is that I had that title and I was the hardest working Miss Great Britain that they ever had, and that they ever will."

At this stage, Deone was introduced into the lion's den in her Miss Great Britain crown and sash which, Zara said, she didn't deserve.

"If it was the other way round and I were in the same situation," Zara said, "I would say that I stand up for women....I wouldn't accept the crown, absolutely no way."

"The point is," Deone interjected, "is that if I didn't take it, it would've been offered to 3rd place, 4th place, 5th place. They say on the night that if for any reason the winner cannot fulfil her duties, the first runner-up will take them on."

"But you don't have to take it," Zara argued.

Deone replied – to applause from the audience - "It was my dream as well as your dream. And you gave it up."

When Katie Price asked what else the pageant focused on apart from looks, Deone replied, "Zara worked really hard to gain that title, she did all her charity work– nobody can ever take that away from her". Addressing her directly, she continued, "But afterwards I think your views and opinions changed on how you wanted to go forward In the future."

The discussion moved on to how Zara found out she had lost her title. "I was so hurt," she said, "I was the last to know, they rang my mum and said they'd put a statement on Twitter saying, 'Don't worry, Zara, we're not taking the title away from you'.

"What was the rush? There was no real rush, no official duties to do, there was only two weeks left of *Love Island*. I've worked so hard, I've attended charity events, I've raised so much money – ".

"Then why would you put all that at risk?" asked an incredulous June Sarpong, at the same time as Deone adding, "Why not wait until next year to go on *Love Island*?"

A clearly riled Zara retorted, "If they were that bothered they should never have let me go on *Love Island* in the first place, end of."

Andrea McLean cut in at this stage. "I really admire that you're a feisty girl and you obviously believe very strongly in sticking up for womens' rights, but part of that belief is sticking up for your own decency," - cue vigorous applause from audience – "but you seem to be blaming everybody else when, at the end of the day, it was only you who did that, so can you not see why people are behaving the way they are towards you?"

"I totally accept what I did and I'm dealing with the consequences right now," Zara replied, "What I'm saying is, is how it was done, how I was treated."

At that point, it was time up and the credits rolled, bringing the tense stand-off to a close.

The encounter had clearly been a humiliation for Zara and, when the cameras stopped rolling and she and Deone were ushered back into the green room, she allowed the defiant smiles to drop.

While being graceful enough to let Deone know that there were no hard feelings, and that she wished her well, she showed no such magnanimity towards her former boss, Kate Solomons-Freakley, whom she was facing for the first time since the whole drama erupted.

When Kate attempted to justify the reason for one of Zara's main bugbears – that the beauty queen hadn't been informed of her de-crowning before it was announced to the public – Zara saw red and a huge argument ensued.

An insider told *The Sun*, "Zara was going ballistic towards Kate, edging closer while pointing and shouting. Her mum and her management had to physically remove her from the green room. She was being extremely aggressive."

Kate later confirmed the story. "She turned to me and said, 'Why are you smiling? Your organisation is a joke!' and that I had made her mum ill with the stress. I told her to calm down, that she was embarrassing herself, but she had completely lost her temper."

Zara hit back on Twitter, denying that she was escorted off the ITV premises: "Never heard such lies in all my life! Ask anyone at ITV!"

Deone was whisked to *The Sun's* offices immediately after *Loose Women* had aired and, during a live Facebook interview, admitted that she had been nervous about coming face to face with Zara.

"I think basically Zara was going on *Loose Women* anyway and obviously with regards to the Miss GB organisation and what had happened, they had not really had their say about it," she said. "So the idea was that we both went on and we could both have our say.

"But it was a little more fiery, shall we say, than I anticipated."

Deone was not without empathy for her former pageant rival. "It's difficult because we were coming from two different stances, and I get why she would be upset. But at the end of the day I'm not the one who has done anything wrong and that's what people are failing to see. I never stole the crown. It was her decision, her choice."

"But yes," she admitted, "I was really, really nervous beforehand – just to sit beside each other and not knowing what was going to happen."

Despite a handful of tweets accusing the panel of bullying her, the tide of support for Zara appeared to have turned followed her *Loose Women* appearance. At this stage, Kate felt able to, finally, say her piece and reveal the real story of what exactly had gone on behind closed doors.

In a two-page spread in *The Sun* – headed "Zara Holland is obsessed with being a celebrity", Kate revealed that when Zara had first been crowned that September, she asked her if she wanted to be successful or famous.

"Zara replied that she wanted to be famous," Kate said. "Although she raised £3,000 for charity in the run-up to Miss Great Britain, her charity work appeared to have stopped as soon as she won. All she wanted to do was appear at high profile red carpet events.

"She begged us to let her go on the TV show *Ex on the Beach*, and we said no. We had a very frank, very harsh conversation about her responsibilities and that she couldn't be associated with sex on television.

"Zara agreed that she would never have sex on TV and complained that the Miss GB bosses were holding her back from achieving her ambitions."

They were therefore stunned and horrified when footage of her *Love Island* tryst was aired to the nation, and when the hashtag #MissBJ started trending on Twitter.

"We work with charities and children," Kate continued. "We can't be associated with a winner who has sex on TV.

"If she had come out of the villa and held her hands up and asked what she could've done to rectify the situation, things could've been different. I'm not saying she would've kept her title, but we could've potentially looked at a different scenario for her. But there was no apology towards us or for letting the Miss GB brand down."

Kate explained that she was initially very happy that Zara showed such respect and appreciation towards her title to begin with and was doing so much to raise its profile. "But in reality she has done nothing more than turn on the very company that worked with her to help her achieve her goals."

Zara's management company responded to the article stating that Zara "would continue to carry out her charity work in private."

Meanwhile, Zara's oft-repeated excuse that she had been drunk in the Hideaway was contradicted by the man she was shown having sex with, Alex Bowen. He tweeted that islanders were only allowed two drinks per night, with an hour in between each. "Her claim that she was drunk made me look really bad, as though I took advantage. But you can't get drunk on *Love Island*, they ration your alcohol.

"Zara is the one who has f***ed it up for herself, she needs to get over it and move on. She had made her bed and now she should lay in it."

Zara remained very much in the news, though not for any of her charity work. She shot a 2017 calendar and landed a role as columnist for *New!* Magazine, before starting filming for ITV2 game show *Release The Hounds* with co-stars Cara de La Hoyde and Nathan Massey, the *Love Island* winners.

Zara admitted she was genuinely remorseful of her actions. Interviewed by *The Sun* to coincide with the launch of the 2017 series of *Love Island* she said that while the experience had made her a stronger person, her on-screen romp was "the biggest mistake of my life – it cost me everything."

And, despite not being present to perform the crowning ceremony, she had some wise words for her Miss Great Britain successor, Ursula Carlton from Aberdeen.

"Ursula needs to steer clear of reality shows," she said. "It's not a good idea if you want to keep your title.

"Reality bites, as they say."

Rima Fakih, Miss USA 2010

"I have a clean record – I was very embarrassed and scared"

The state of Michigan can lay claim to two significant pageant firsts: it produced the first black Miss USA and, twenty years later, the first Muslim Miss USA.

The Miss USA pageant on the whole, though, trailed some way behind the Miss America contest in crowning such noteworthy winners.

Vanessa Williams – now a star of stage and screen – became the first black Miss America in 1983, but it wasn't until 1990 that Michigan's Carol Gist took the Miss USA title and made headlines for the same reason. It was a successful year for pageantry in the States: Carol finished first runner-up at Miss Universe, while her Miss USA runner-up, Gina Marie Tolleson, went on to win the Miss World title.

Carol's win opened the door for eight more black women to take the crown to date, including Kenya Moore (later a star of *The Real Housewives of Atlanta*) in 1993, and Chelsi Smith (who called herself bi-racial) becoming, in 1995, the first Miss USA to win Miss Universe in 15 years.

Yet when Rima Fakih was crowned the first Muslim Miss USA in 2010, her win wasn't welcomed with quite such enthusiasm in some quarters, and even less so as her year of office spiralled into a series of less than flattering stories about her conduct, culminating in her arrest for drink driving after she had handed over the crown.

In many ways, 25-year-old Rima was the very definition of a new generation of beauty queen. Born in Lebanon, her family moved to New York when she was eight years old. They settled in an Arab-American community in Dearborn, Michigan, regarded as the capital of Muslim America, where Rima earned a degree in economics and business management.

Prior to winning the Miss USA pageant, Rima had represented Michigan in the Miss Lebanese Emigrant contest, open to those of Lebanese origin living overseas. She finished third overall before taking the Miss Michigan USA title and going on to make history by becoming the first Muslim to triumph in the Miss USA final in May 2010.

Asked on stage after her win how she felt, the brunette quipped, "Ask me after I've had a pizza! I feel great." Turning to the then owner of the Miss USA pageant she added, "Thanks for hiring me, Donald Trump!"

It was inevitable that there would be so much emphasis on Rima's background. She had indicated prior to the pageant that some of those in her Michigan community of Dearborn "may be a little on the strict side," adding, "but my family in general is not."

But while her own community was largely positive about her win, right-wing America was less so. Radio host Debbie Schlussel said Rima won due to the "politically-correct, Islamo-pandering climate," labelling her a "Lebanese Muslim Hezbollah supporter with relatives who are top terrorists."

Right-wing pundit Michelle Malkin went further, ranting that Rima's supporters "were too busy tooting the identity politics horn to care what comes out of her mouth."

Even former Miss America Gretchen Carlson, now a *Fox News* anchor, alleged that Rima won purely because of the "PC society" they lived in.

One of Rima's chief supporters rushed to her defence. "This is a real face of Arab Americans," he said, "not the stereotypes you hear about. We have culture. We have beauty. We have history – and today we made history. She believed in her dreams."

Another supporter compared the importance of Rima's win to that of Barack Obama becoming the first African American President, while a third said, "This is far better than hearing that a Muslim has carried out a terrorist attack. It is 2010 – we don't all have camels and live in tents."

Yet some in the Muslim community disagreed that she was a proper representative of the community. Shia Muslim scholar Ghazal Omar said, "To say that she is a Muslim is inaccurate. No Muslim woman can call herself a Muslim and be on stage in a bikini."

Rima's own opinions were keenly sought by the media, and in one of her first interviews she told reporters that she came from "more of a spiritual family. Religion doesn't define me or my family. My family has been very liberal, and we respect all different kinds of religion. We celebrate both Christian and Muslim holidays.

"I'd like to say I'm American first, and I am an Arab-American, I am Lebanese-American, and I am Muslim-American.

"It is absolutely false that my family is connected to Hezbollah. Once again that's just a stereotype. I hope everyone can look beyond the beauty pageant stereotype too and see that what I'm doing represents the United States as a country of opportunity, where you can do anything you want to, and where ethnicity and religion cannot stop you."

So far, so inspirational, yet just days later, pictures from 2007 were uncovered showing Rima in red shorts, a tank top and towering stilettos, allegedly taken during her participation in a "Stripper 101" pole-dancing contest.

The host of Detroit's *Mojo in the Morning* radio show, which organised the contest, told *ABC News* that the Miss Universe organisation had called, asking for more photos and information about the event their new Miss USA had taken part in.

"They couldn't tell us what their intentions were," the DJ said, "and we didn't want to give them anything that may have caused her to relinquish her crown.

"But it's ridiculous because in these photos she is wearing more clothes than she was in the photos for the pageant."

The pole-dancing contest, run by professional strippers, required the contestants to wear 'comfortable clothes', while the winner was awarded with jewellery, 'adult toys' and a stripper's pole to take home.

Mojo in the Morning confirmed that the photos had been on their website for three years and in an interview with *Fox News*, Rima explained that they were taken at a promotional event, not at the pole-dancing contest. "My friend suggested I get up there and give it a try, so I did. And a few pictures were snapped, and not from the best angle," she laughed.

Miss USA pageant officials investigated the photos, and allowed her to keep her crown. "They were fair enough to look into the situation and see that it was just a class," said Rima. "It was something innocent that was taken into something else."

Just before setting off to Las Vegas for the Miss Universe pageant in August, Rima spoke out about plans to build a mosque close by to Ground Zero, the site of the 9/11 terrorist attacks on the World Trade Center in 2001.

Rima told the *Inside Edition* news programme that the plans to build a $100m mosque and community centre two blocks away from Ground Zero was insensitive. "I totally agree with President Obama with the statement on Constitutional rights of freedom of religion," she said. "But I also agree that it shouldn't be so close to the World Trade Center. We should be more concerned with the tragedy than with religion."

More eyebrows were raised when Rima arrived for the Miss Universe pageant and the finalists were given the option to pose topless –

covered in body paint - for their official contestant photo shoot. Rima chose to do so, albeit with her painted back towards the camera.

It was a compromise, Rima explained. "I like to do the back," she told *The Detroit News*. "I didn't want to do the front for many reasons. I'm an Arab, I'm a Muslim, and I didn't want to disappoint people. I apologise if I disrespected anyone."

Rima chose her national costume as a tribute to Barack Obama and it was commissioned by the *Victoria's Secrets* Fashion Show designer Martin Izquierdo. Inspired by the bald eagle Seal of the President of the United States, the skimpy feathered leotard came complete with golden wings and was unveiled by the beauty queen on a YouTube video. "Mr President," she said, "the amazing costume I will wear represents the celebration of life, liberty and all that is American – a tribute to your work to bring peace to the world."

Despite her high profile during the build-up to the pageant, Rima became the first Miss USA to miss out on a spot in the Miss Universe semi-final for eight years.

Rima returned to the apartment in New York that she shared for a year with the current Miss Universe, and continued with her reign. But that reign was nearly brought to a premature end due to her taste for clubs and partying.

Earlier in her year of office she had overslept and missed a TV interview after a heavy night out with friends, causing Miss Universe President Paula Shurgart to send Rima home to Michigan for a few weeks to decide if she wanted to carry on as Miss USA.

The reins had been tightened on their winners since Miss USA 2006 Tara Conner came perilously close to losing her crown for alleged drug use and underage drinking. Tara – whose story was covered in full in *Misdemeanours* Vol 1 – was only saved when owner Donald Trump gave her a second chance on the condition that she went to rehab after her reign was over.

When Rima seemed to be heading in the same direction, Paula Shugart ordered her to speak to Tara for some advice about trying to keep out of trouble.

"Rima said that talking to Tara was very helpful," Paula told *Fox News*. "Keep in mind, whoever wins goes to New York and their entire world is packed up and they live no expenses for a year. You meet a lot of famous people and can get caught up in that. Rima said it helped her learn that you can't fool all of us, and Tara said that it makes it easier if you just tell the truth."

But with just under a fortnight of her reign remaining, Rima went on another all-night bender. She lied to the organisation about what time she had come in, causing them to request a copy of the CCTV security tapes, where the truth of her arrival home at 4am was exposed.

"There was one night last week when she had some interviews the next day," explained Paula. "First we thought she was at the apartment and someone was trying to get her to the interview. She was sound asleep and looked like she had been out all night. She made the interviews, but we did ask about the security tapes, as it's a serious business, especially after Tara.

"We usually like to keep a handle on them," she added. "Their apartment is next to the office so it is hard for them to get out and do things without us knowing about them."

Paula had praise for Rima, though. "She has been an incredible titleholder," she said. "She goes 100% on everything, and definitely keeps you on your toes."

With an almost audible sigh of relief, she finished by saying, "She is crowning her successor soon, so maybe she went out to blow off some steam."

With a week to go before Rima relinquished her title, she appeared on the *Good Morning America* programme to discuss her rocky year. "I'm proud to say I'll be giving up my crown on June 19," she said, adding with a knowing smile, "And I'm proud that I still have my crown."

Asked if her relaxed behaviour was due to her coming to the end of her reign, she replied, "You have to look at the beginning of my reign: the attacks and the controversy that I wasn't prepared for – 'You're the first Arab, you're the first Muslim, do you think you're a real Miss USA?'

"Then you had those racy pictures which were just a pole-dancing class and portrayed as something else. Then you went from the mosque controversy to body paint, and then, you know, people didn't like that I was on the *WWE Tough Enough* reality show. But I think everything has calmed down since then, and here I am today!"

Asked about whether Miss USA should be allowed to stay out until 4am, Rima replied, "I want to clarify that Miss USA is a real woman, not this, like 'world peace'. She's a real human being who has her own opinion, is an adult and can make some mature decisions. But you're right, though – staying out late if you have work the next day, you should be responsible."

Laughing, she added, "But let's look on the bright side – I wasn't doing anything illegal."

How those words must have come back to haunt her when, six months after relinquishing her crown, Rima was arrested on a charge of drink driving.

"I went out with some old friends and we were having fun," she said in an interview with *E! News*. "A couple of them were very intoxicated, so when we went to leave I wouldn't let them drive. So when I got pulled over, I was the driver."

The police officer involved stated that Rima was driving at 60mph and weaving in and out of traffic on a Michigan highway when she was pulled over. A breathalyser test found her more than twice the legal limit, with an uncorked, half-empty bottle of champagne behind the driver's seat.

Rima, said the officer, immediately identified herself as Miss USA but denied she had been drinking. She was taken to a police cell 'until she was sober for her safety and the safety of others', and while there she sent out a message on Twitter saying, "Let's clear things up now...I'm NOT in Michigan and I'm NOT in jail! Wrong Fakih."

The tweets were removed almost immediately and Rima told *E! News*, "I was afraid for my family and that the news could get to my family. It was a bad idea but too late anyway. It was everywhere in minutes.

"I have a clean record," she continued. "I was very embarrassed and scared."

Rima, who was facing a maximum of 93 days in prison, appeared in court the following April and pleaded no contest to the charge of driving while visibly impaired. She was sentenced the following month to six months' probation, 20 hours of community service, and ordered to pay $600 in costs.

Outside the courtroom, Rima was clearly relieved. "You learn, you pay your price for making mistakes and you move on. I'm very happy I can put this behind me," she told reporters.

Two months later, she appeared to have learned that lesson when gossip website *TMZ* filmed her staggering out of a Hollywood nightclub in an obviously highly intoxicated state. Spotting the camera she yelled, "*TMZ,* I'm not driving!"

It was four years until Rima made headlines again, when the first Muslim Miss USA converted to Christianity, ahead of her wedding to Lebanese-Canadian music producer Wassim Salibi, better known as Tony Sal, manager of R&B singer The Weeknd.

Rima's decision to follow Jesus caused an outcry on social media among some Muslims, assuring her that this move would "send her straight to Hell".

The star-studded wedding took place in Lebanon in May 2016, with Rima looking every inch a queen in her gown made for her by Lebanese designer Elie Saab and, according to some reports, taking 1846 hours to make by 45 people, at a cost of half a million dollars.

Having settled down to married life in Beverly Hills, California, Rima and Tony announced the birth of their first child in January 2017, a daughter they named Rima after her mum.

Tony was the proudest of fathers. "I'm now in love with two Rimas," he joked.

Protest, Politics & Pageantry

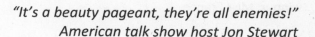

> *"It's a beauty pageant, they're all enemies!"*
> *American talk show host Jon Stewart*

In the smash hit movie *Miss Congeniality*, undercover FBI agent Gracie Hart (played by Sandra Bullock) competes in the Miss United States pageant in a bid to prevent a bomb attack that threatens to disrupt the event.

Interviewed on stage by host Stan Fields (William Shatner) Gracie is asked what she considers the one most important thing needed in today's society.

She answers, "Harder punishment for parole violators, Stan". The audience sits in bemused silence, until Gracie remembers that she is meant to be a beauty queen, not an undercover cop, and quickly adds, "And world peace!" - to ecstatic applause from the crowd.

As demonstrated so well in *Miss Congeniality*, a heartfelt desire for world peace became a stereotypical and clichéd mantra for politically correct pageant contestants the world over, yet history shows that many bridges must be built before even a beauty pageant itself becomes a battle-free zone.

On the very day the British government signed an agreement in Cairo to withdraw its forces from its Suez Canal base, Miss Egypt won the Miss World title in London.

Yet 19th October 1954 marked a notable victory for 21 year old Antigone Costanda and for Egypt in more ways than one. Antigone had actually won the Miss Egypt title the year before, but her family was unable to afford to fund her trip to London to take part in the 1953 Miss World contest.

Instead, her place was taken by runner-up Marina Papaelia, whose outspoken antics in London were recounted in *Misdemeanours* Vol 1. Marina, furious at being placed only third in Miss World, shouted, "I theenk she steenk!" before collapsing on stage at the feet of the winner, Miss France.

Original winner Antigone was not pleased at missing her chance to go to Miss World, and told the *Daily Express*, "Marina was second to me in Miss Egypt and had no right to the title. I am claiming damages from the organisers."

Eric Morley responded by saying, "Miss Costanda will qualify for Miss World next year – if she has calmed down by then."

The Egyptian Tourism Department agreed that funding her trip would be a worthwhile investment for their country – a decision which turned out to be a very wise one, when Antigone, whose family ran a grocery store, beat 15 other finalists to the Miss World title. Yet it seemed only the judges – which included singer Gracie Fields – and her fellow countrymen were pleased with the result.

The *Daily Express* reported that her rival contestants were left 'seething'. Miss Sweden told journalists that Antigone was "too fat in the face and hips. She knows how to smile, but is not beautiful." Miss Germany, meanwhile, complained that the winner "wobbles too much, like Marilyn Monroe."

Antigone shrugged off the criticism and said, "It was luck. I'm very happy, it was an adventure."

Her adventure did not extend to being invited to London a year later to crown her successor, the situation between Egypt and the UK being deemed too hostile for her to return. The 1955 winner was crowned by British actress Eunice Gayson instead.

Politics really began to bite at the Miss World organisation in 1956, in its sixth year of existence.

"You think the politicians get trouble," said organiser Eric Morley, when faced with pairing contestants as room-mates. "You should hear from me!"

Despite the 1954 withdrawal, Western forces had just invaded Egypt again in a bid to regain control of the Suez Canal and to remove the Egyptian President, a decision history now concludes "signified the end of Great Britain's role as one of the world's major powers", and forced the resignation of British Prime Minister Anthony Eden.

Eric Morley's problem was no longer purely working out who spoke which language, but whom to pair with whom to avoid any diplomatic incident.

"I usually sort them out so they can understand one another," he said. "Then I discover that their politics clash. If it isn't the Suez Canal, it's Cyprus or the Gaza Strip. I can't put Miss Egypt with the British girl, and I can't put her with Miss Israel, either."

Miss USA didn't pose a problem at all, said Morley. "You can room Americans with anyone. I think I'll put her with Miss South Africa."

But in the end, Britain's Iris Waller agreed to share with Norma Dugo, Miss Egypt, after the pageant sponsors emphasised the importance of maintaining diplomatic relations.

"The girls say beauty comes before politics," Morley told the press. "They don't care if the Suez Canal dries up."

The Egyptian government spared Morley one future headache at least: they withdrew from future Miss World contests until 1988.

Spain's ongoing dispute with the UK over ownership of the British colony of Gibraltar caused many an upset at Miss World over the years. General Franco claimed that the Rock was legally part of Spain and he refused to recognise a Gibraltar government.

Spain first withdrew from the pageant in 1965 when Miss Gibraltar, Rosemarie Vinales, refused to go home. "I'm disappointed that Miss Spain has withdrawn," she said, "I wanted to compete against her."

That vanishing Miss Spain, Alicia Borras, is now one of her country's most famous mature models, and at the age of 69 modelled for both *Harpers Bazaar* and on the catwalk at the 2015 Madrid Fashion Week shows.

At Miss World 1965, Syrian officials complained to the organisers that Miss Israel had dared speak to Miss Syria to say hello at the introductory session, despite their countries being at war.

Miss Israel, Shlomit Gat, walked over to Miss Syria, Raymonde Doucco, and said, "Don't you think it would be nice if I said hello, even though our countries aren't talking?" At that point, Miss Syria burst into tears and fled to the side of her chaperone, sobbing, "I can't talk to her, I can't – and I don't want to! I've had instructions not to talk to her!"

Miss Israel was baffled, telling reporters, "I can't understand this silly behaviour. After all, it's only a beauty contest, not a summit meeting."

The 1966 contest saw a repeat of events a year earlier when Miss Spain, Paquita Torres Perez, withdrew due to the presence of Miss Gibraltar, Grace Valverde. In an interesting footnote, Grace was one of three members of the same family to be crowned Miss Gibraltar. Her daughter, Michelle Torres, won in 1992, and her niece, Melanie Chipolina, took the crown in 2005.

Jordan took part in eight Miss World finals, the last of which was in 1966, when Vera Jalil Khamis, a Palestinian Christian from East Jerusalem, represented the kingdom in London. Just months later the Miss Jordan contest was cancelled indefinitely by the Ministry of Tourism due to the Arab-Israeli war of 1967, and to this day the pageant has never been revived.

India boycotted the 1967 contest in a protest concerning the Vietnam War. India's Reita Faria won the Miss World title in 1966 and, as was traditional for the winners of that era, joined comedian Bob Hope on a tour of Vietnam to entertain the US troops stationed there. The Indian government was a supporter of the Ho Chi Minh's Communist government in North Vietnam, and a spokesman called Reita's visit "a considerable embarrassment to our country. Many people at home were extremely upset because the Vietnam issue is one in which any citizen of our country should not interfere."

The Indian government refused to send a contestant to the 1967 final, although Reita Faria was allowed to attend in order to crown her successor.

Miss USA Pamela Pall also faced opposition to the Vietnam War when organisers were tipped off about a potential attempt by students to kidnap her while the contestants were visiting Cambridge. The route of their tour was changed to foil the plot, and Pamela told the press, "I had no idea of the threat – it is a great shock to me."

After a three-year boycott by Spain, the country returned to Miss World in 1968. But Maria Amparo Lorenza had barely unpacked her suitcase before she became the next in line to quit due to old wounds re-opening with her Gibraltan nemesis.

Miss Gibraltar, Sandra Sanguinetti, allegedly remarked that the presence of Miss Spain in the contest was proof that they accepted the Rock to be British. Despite Sandra later denying she had said anything so inflammatory, Miss Spain disappeared from the pageant hotel in London for several hours and missed the dress rehearsal, before returning and promising to stay on if her rival apologised.

Sandra refused, saying, "I have nothing to apologise for. Miss Spain is my friend, only yesterday we had coffee together."

Miss Spain reacted by quitting the competition immediately, telling Spanish reporters, "As an Andalusian, the British flag over the Rock offends me."

Furious Miss World chiefs fired off a complaint to the organisers of the Miss Gibraltar pageant.

Jean Gibbons, of Mecca, wrote to the Gibraltar Tourist Board saying, "If you wish to send Miss Gibraltar to the Miss World contest next year, may we please have your assurance that she will reply 'No comment' to any questions asked of a political nature."

As a result, the Gibraltar Tourist Board issued an edict that the 1969 Miss Gibraltar, Marilou Chiappe, would be gagged from talking about any sticky issue. This demand proved particularly important that year when Spanish ruler General Franco ordered that the border between Spain and Gibraltar should be closed in 1969. The frontier didn't open again fully – even after his death in 1975 – until 13th December 1982, meaning that for 13 years friends and family were forced to make a day-long journey by sea to visit each other.

The 1968 pageant had already proved a headache for Mecca, when they had been faced with Miss Lebanon Lili Bisson who, at the age of 15, was two years below the minimum age limit of 17. They barred her from actually being judged as a contestant, but allowed her to stay in London and take part in the show on television.

That year's Miss USA, Johnny Avery, kicked up a fuss once the contest was over, accusing the judges of being interested only in Vietnam and even alleging that one pageant official called her a "warmonger" and "a rapist of little countries". Johnny, who failed to make the final 15, added, "The whole contest is tinged with politics – over half the judges were British."

Johnny had found the build-up to the final just as vexing. "I feel like an animal," she told the press as the girls lined up for swimwear photos. "I just hate the way men stand around comparing and criticising us."

Miss Ireland 1971, June Glover, caused a security alert at the Miss World finals when it was discovered that she was from Northern Ireland. The Troubles – the thirty-year conflict between Protestants and Catholics with the constitutional status of Northern Ireland at its centre - was at its height at that time, and Mecca laid on extra security as a result of June's disclosure.

Both she and Miss Australia had fallen foul of Mecca's rules, in that the contestant or her father must have been born in the country they were representing. Miss Australia, Valerie Roberts, was revealed to be an Essex girl born, like her dad, in Chingford, before emigrating to Oz when she was 12.

Julia Morley allowed both the girls to stay, saying, "Our rules are made to be broken. It would be a tragedy if a girl is sent home on a technicality, a mistake made by us when we drew up the rules."

Mrs Morley promised an overhaul of the residency rules a year later and she was as good as her word: from 1972, contestants would qualify if they had lived in a country for a minimum of five years.

Following the flour bomb protests the year before, the Miss World organisation took the unprecedented decision in 1971 not to sell tickets for the final to the general public. Instead they were distributed to patrons of Mecca bingo halls in order to try and foil a repeat of the previous year's disruption.

Miss Lebanon, Georgina Rizk, failed to make the final 15 at Miss World 1970, but was crowned Miss Universe 1971 just months later. However, she was denied the opportunity to hand over her title a year later, due to a major incident in Israel shortly beforehand.

Sixteen Puerto Rican pilgrims, on their way to the Holy Land, were murdered by Japanese terrorists allegedly hired by Palestinian guerrillas in a massacre at Tel Aviv airport in May 1972. As a result, Georgina's exit permit to travel from Lebanon to Puerto Rico for the Miss Universe 1972 pageant was refused her for security reasons, nor was a Lebanese contestant allowed to take part in the contest.

It was destined to be a year of terrorism on a mass scale.

In September 1972, just four months after the Tel Aviv attack, eleven Israeli athletes were taken hostage by Palestinian terrorists at the Summer Olympics in Munich. All eleven were later killed during a botched rescue attempt at a nearby airport.

The organisers of the 1972 Miss International pageant in Japan one month later were forced to ban Miss Israel, Ronit Gafni, from competing due to security scares caused by both terror attacks. Security chiefs for the pageant uncovered a plot in which Tokyo students were plotting to kidnap Miss Israel, in exchange for the jailing of a Japanese terrorist after the Tel Aviv airport massacre.

Miss Lebanon was also barred from the competition.

In an extraordinary twist, Georgina Rizk – the Lebanese Miss Universe winner - went on to marry Ali Hassan Salameh, who was then chief of operations for Black September, the group responsible for the Munich Olympics massacre. He was assassinated by Mossad in 1979.

The Miss World organisers didn't go so far as to ban Miss Israel from competing at their 1972 pageant in London three months after the Olympics terrorist attack, but security measures surrounding the event were the most stringent they had ever been.

No fewer than 17 security personnel were sent to London Airport to meet Miss Israel, Hannah Ordan, from her El Al flight for the contest. "You can't mix beauty contests with politics," said the 17-year-old student. "I will be quite safe."

"This year's Miss World has become more like an ordeal," said a Mecca spokesman. "The girls are guarded 24 hours a day and escorted by armed guards on their trips between their hotel and the Albert Hall for rehearsals."

When in 1973 the Miss Universe pageant moved to Europe for the first time in its history, it came under even more intense pressure from security concerns and local demands. Held in Athens, the Greek authorities issued a crackdown on the contestants exposing too much flesh during the ten-day pageant, no easy task during one of the worst heatwaves in Greece for years.

An archaeological society imposed a ban on the swimwear round, due to the final being held at one of the sites under its supervision, the ancient Odeon of Herod Atticus theatre, at the foot of the Acropolis.

Miss Israel, Linor Schriebman, found herself under constant guard from both Greek and Israeli security agents, who insisted on accompanying her to costume fittings and demanded a bedroom next to hers at the pageant hotel. A spokesman confirmed the necessity of such close scrutiny. "Due to the Olympic tragedy in Munich," she said, "they have to be extraordinarily protective."

A diplomatic incident was narrowly avoided in 1975 when Cuba's first – and to date only – Miss World delegate arrived in London. It was soon discovered that Marisela Maxie Clark was a naturalised American who had not lived in Cuba since her family fled to Miami when she was 7 years old.

The First Secretary at the Cuban Embassy told the *Daily Mail*, "We do not recognise her. She is American now and Cuba has not taken part in any of these contests since Fidel Castro took over as President in 1959."

Maxie had, in fact, won the Miss Cuba Libre (Miss *Free Cuba*) title in Miami, but was accepted by the Miss World office as their official representative, and went on to win fourth place in the final.

When Rina Messinger became the first Israeli woman to be crowned Miss Universe in 1976, she presented the organisers with what they called a 'monumental security problem'. Their main task was to protect her from pro-Palestinian guerrillas during the extensive travel plans and personal appearances she would make in her year of office.

Rina herself was unperturbed. "There are many people who are not political and don't read about politics," she said. "I will tell them about Israel in my own way. I am not afraid of kidnapping or violence."

Despite Rina's defiance, Israeli secret servicemen travelled with her throughout her reign.

Argentina withdrew from the Miss World contest in 1982 due to military conflict with the UK. The Falklands War was a ten-week battle between Argentinian and British forces for ownership of the Falkland Islands, South Georgia and the South Sandwich Islands. The UK retained its territory when Argentina surrendered, and relations between the two countries remained fraught for many years, with Miss Argentina staying away from Miss World until 1987.

In 1993, the Lebanese authorities threatened arrest of its Miss World representative, Ghada El Turk, when a media agency circulated a photo of her locking arms with Miss Israel, Tamara Porat, at a gathering of contestants in Johannesburg. She faced legal proceedings because Lebanon was still technically at war with Israel, which occupied a strip of southern Lebanon.

"Our beauty queen might have to stand trial because she did this in spite of strict Arab boycott regulations against Israel," said Lebanon's Minister of Tourism, while the country's top public prosecutor confirmed that she faced a charge of "collaborating with the enemy."

Despite Ghada's assertion that she didn't realise she was standing next to Miss Israel in the photograph, it was four months before she was allowed back into her country.

"According to the information we obtained, Miss Lebanon did not have bad intentions that would cause her to be stripped of her title or to be punished," said Michel Pharaon, Lebanon's Tourism minister, in a televised press conference. "Miss Lebanon has been the subject of a racist and random campaign," he continued. "I say that we should support her."

American talk show host Jon Stewart joked, "It's a beauty pageant. They're all enemies!"

In the event, neither Miss Israel nor Miss Lebanon made the Top 15 of the Miss World pageant.

In 1996, the Miss World final took place to a backdrop of the most violent and extreme protests yet witnessed in a beauty pageant, making the flour bombs of the 1970 contest seem like child's play in comparison.

When it was announced that the contest would take place in Bangalore, India, the news caused widespread fury among the mainly Hindu population, and the two months leading up to the final saw protest after protest in the streets of the cities. A man in southern India died after he set himself on fire in protest at what he and many thousands of others considered to be an event not just demeaning to women, but one which undermined India's 5,000-year cultural heritage.

In an attempt to appease the protesters, the swimwear section of the pageant was moved to the Seychelles, after its government offered to pay $5.3m to the Indian company organising the contest.

On the night of the final itself in Bangalore, 1,500 people were arrested and seven policemen injured, though heavy security kept those inside the venue free from immediate harm.

Two years later, Miss Israel Ilanit Levy modelled a bullet-proof evening gown in the Miss Universe final, to send a message that 'life goes on', despite months of violence between Israel and Palestine.

The Miss Universe pageant returned to the Mediterranean in 2000, this time to Cyprus, and found that the problems they encountered were not far removed from their Greek visit in 1973.

Priests of the Cypriot Orthodox Church lambasted the pageant for its "evil, soul-destroying ways", seeking to "demean women and destroy marriages."

Father Marios asked, "How can an island that has been partitioned by war, which has missing people and mothers who cry themselves to sleep, so happily promote half-naked women?"

However, the Greek-Cypriot government had spent £5m of taxpayers' money on the event, a decision the Minister for Tourism defended keenly. "Who said anything about culture? This is not culture. It is entertainment, pure and simple."

Yet it seemed not all of his fellow Cypriots agreed with him. Miss Universe organisers were forced to slash ticket prices by 60% due to indifference from the locals. The government of Cyprus had already caused upset in France by asking The Louvre Museum to lend them the original statue of Venus de Milo, a request immediately quashed.

Turkey announced it would not be sending a candidate to an island it invaded in 1974, while the Chinese authorities were furious that a contestant was calling herself Miss Taiwan, an area which China considered part of their territory.

The fallout from the terrorist attacks on the World Trade Center on 11th September 2001 reverberated around the pageant world.

The organisers of the 2002 Miss Egypt pageant debated as to whether to cancel their contest as a result of the increased threat of terrorism, before deciding to hastily arrange a pageant of just nine contestants, won by the previous year's runner up, Sally Shaheen.

The 2002 Miss Universe final was held in Puerto Rico, and Miss Trinidad & Tobago – a Muslim - caused a stir of her own. Muslim groups from the islands objected to their contestant, branding Nasma Mohammed "an embarrassment to the faith."

"We have to be careful how we organise events," said Miss Universe spokesman Mary Hilliard, "and who we match as room-mates, even who we put together for photos.

"Miss Lebanon isn't here this year," she confirmed. "Her national pageant director didn't think it was right to have her spend three weeks in the same hotel as Miss Israel and Miss Egypt".

Miss Israel herself regretted the withdrawal of her fellow competitor. "It's very bad that Miss Lebanon didn't come," she said. "This is my first time out of the Middle East and I was scared." But she said she was friends with Miss Egypt, despite organisers keeping them apart due to ongoing tensions between their countries.

As a result of the 11th September attacks, more security guards were employed than usual at that year's pageant. Both Miss Egypt and Miss Israel had received threats since arriving in San Juan, and bomb-sniffing dogs made regular sweeps of the delegates' hotel. All deliveries were seized and examined by security guards.

Due to disputes over the island of Cyprus, Miss Turkey and Miss Cyprus were also kept apart. The north of Cyprus has been Turkish-occupied, and the south Greek-Cypriot controlled, since the Turkish invasion of the island in 1974.

Miss Turkey was having none of it. "We are all different cultures here together, and I want to show this is also possible in politics," said Cagla Kubat.

Mary Hilliard also revealed why she always put Miss Philippines and Miss India in separate rooms. "They always bring too many suitcases!" she laughed.

Theresa Beyer, Vice-President of the Miss Universe Organisation, said they couldn't expect to achieve world peace. "We're not that powerful," she said. "All we can say is that in this place, at this moment in time, we have 75 nations represented, they have been able to put aside every difference, and after three weeks a genuine bond has formed."

At the 2002 Miss Universe pageant, Miss Lebanon, Christina Sawaya, refused to attend due to the presence of Miss Israel. Yet it didn't stop her taking part in – and winning - the Miss International pageant a few months later, despite Israel also being represented on stage.

As documented in *Misdemeanours* Volume 1, the Miss World organisation's decision to stage the 2002 pageant In Nigeria caused the biggest loss of life in the history of pageants. Over 200 people were killed in the riots, forcing the organisation and its contestants to flee back to London.

Several contestants, including those from Austria, Denmark, Iceland, Korea, Sri Lanka and Switzerland, had already withdrawn from the pageant in protest of the death sentence by stoning given to Amina Lawal, a Nigerian woman accused of adultery.

When the hot favourite to win the 2010 Miss World crown finished only fourth, there were mutterings of political foul play at work. The pageant was hosted by the Chinese island of Hainan, and there was speculation that the judges had bowed to pressure from Beijing to ensure that the highly-tipped Miss Norway didn't win the crown.

The Chinese government remained furious with Norway after the Oslo-based Nobel Peace Prize committee awarded the prize to the imprisoned Chinese dissident Liu Xioabo a month earlier.

With Beijing and Tokyo also embroiled in arguments over the disputed Diaoyu Islands in the East China Sea, Miss Japan was greeted in near-silence by the audience in the auditorium when she paraded on stage.

Back at Miss Universe, Chinese authorities intervened in 2003 when Chen Szu-yu joined the pageant In Panama with her Miss Taiwan sash. It was the first time in pageant history that an official Miss China had competed alongside Miss Taiwan, resulting in the government of the People's Republic of China ordering that Miss Taiwan be known as Miss Chinese Taipei.

Taiwan is officially known as the Republic of China, but mainland China – the People's Republic of China – does not recognise it as a state, and insists that it competes at international events and forums under the name Chinese Taipei.

The beauty queen was photographed with her two sashes, tearfully telling the media that she wanted to be known as Miss Taiwan. A compromise was finally agreed upon: Chen Szu-yu could wear her Miss Taiwan sash off-stage, but be seen as Miss Chinese Taipei during on stage rehearsals and in the grand final.

Miss World had already succumbed to orders as early as 1998, when Miss Republic of China was told to be renamed as Miss Chinese Taipei. Neither Miss Universe nor Miss World have since allowed a contestant to compete as Miss Taiwan.

Miss Kosovo and Miss Serbia caused consternation when they posed together for a photo during the 2011 Miss Universe pageant preparations. Kosovo declared its independence in 2008, but upon publication of the photo, the Serbian government was quick to confirm that this did not mean that it recognised Kosovo as a country in its own right, still considering it very much part of its territory.

When the Miss Universe pageant moved to Russia in 2013, there was no pretending that it wasn't an international political event.

Miss Kosovo was unable to attend. With the Russian Federation not recognising Kosovo as an independent state, it wasn't able to issue her with a visa. Miss Georgia and Miss Albania both withdrew due to strained relations with Russia, while the pageant itself risked boycott from spectators and sponsors due to Russia's reputation for being both racist and homophobic.

Andy Cohen, an openly gay American TV personality who had hosted the 2012 pageant, boycotted the 2013 show due to Russia's anti-gay stance. "Their discriminatory policies make it unsafe for the gays who live there and the gays coming to work or visit," he told *E! News*. "The law is that anyone under suspicion of homosexuality can be arrested. I don't feel right as a gay man stepping foot in Russia."

Cohen's place as host was taken by MSNBC anchor Thomas Roberts, another openly gay man, who wanted his presence in Moscow to "make a difference."

"Boycotting and vilifying from the outside is too easy," he wrote on his website. "Rather, I choose to offer my support of the LGBT community in Russia by going to Moscow and hosting this event as a journalist, an anchor and a man who happens to be gay. Let people see I am no different to anyone else."

The first ever Miss Myanmar – from the nation formerly known as Burma - took to the stage in Russia, as did the first black Miss Israel.

The 2013 Miss World pageant didn't escape political ructions either that year. The contest was originally to be held in Jakarta, the capital of Indonesia, but Muslim protesters forced the organisers to move it to the less extremist island of Bali.

Hundreds of protesters had taken to the streets in cities across Indonesia, waving banners reading "Reject Miss World", and "Miss World is a whore contest". Some brought goats wearing sashes in an attempt to ridicule the event, while for others who burned effigies of the organisers, it was far more serious.

The Islamic Defenders Front, a hardline group with a long record of vandalising nightspots, hurling stones at western embassies and attacking rival religious groups, had pledged to disrupt the event, leading to the last-minute decision to move the final to Bali.

The British Foreign Office issued a warning, that: "Extremists may be planning attacks targeting the Miss World pageant being held in Bali, including possibly against hotels used by participants."

Miss World Chairman Julia Morley announced that all contestants would wear sarongs over their swimwear, in order to show 'respect' to their hosts.

Indonesia has long been a detractor of beauty pageants. Muslim leaders urged the government to disown Miss Indonesia 1983, Titi Dwijayanti, for daring to represent her country in the Miss World contest in London.

A beauty queen 'selfie' turned ugly at the 2015 Miss Universe pageant, making worldwide news and sending shockwaves across the Middle East.

In a repeat of the events of 22 years earlier, Miss Israel, Doron Matalon, was seen posing for a photograph with Miss Lebanon, Saly Griege, during preparations for the pageant in Florida in January 2015.

Some Lebanese people were incensed, with reportedly 3,000 people calling on social media for their beauty queen to be stripped of her title for daring to consort with the enemy.

"You do not represent Lebanon!" tweeted one angry fellow countryman, while Lebanese journalist and women's rights activist Jumana Haddad told the BBC that the reaction "was to be expected. We are often at war with Israel," she said. "It is not appropriate to pose laughing with those who we consider the enemy."

Despite the border between the two countries being mainly peaceful since the conflict in 2006, technically they were still at war, and the Lebanese were still threatened with a prison sentence if they travelled to Israel. All Israeli products were also still banned in Lebanon, and contact between people from opposing factions was illegal.

Saly Griege rushed to defend herself, telling her followers on her Instagram site that she had been 'pestered' by Miss Israel for a photo, before finally being 'photobombed' by her – in other words, including her in a photo without her knowledge or permission.

"Since the first day of my arrival to participate in Miss Universe, I was very cautious to avoid being in any photo or communication with Miss Israel, who tried several times to take a photo with me," Saly said. "I was having a photo with Miss Japan and Miss Slovenia, suddenly Miss Israel jumped in and took a selfie, and uploaded it on her social media."

Saly's agent, Richard Pharaon, went further, telling the press that, "it was 100% deliberate. I can confirm that it was organised and planned since November 2014. Miss Israel was trying from the beginning to reach Saly and to have a selfie with her during the 20 days they stayed there.

"They were both sitting together once at the Marriott Hotel and Miss Israel came and asked Saly to have a selfie with her. Saly refused, of course, since she's perfectly aware of the conflict with Israel, and the whole situation in Lebanon."

He also made it clear that there had been no interaction between the two contestants since the selfie was taken. "They're not friends, they're not roommates, they don't like each other and there's no interaction between them," Pharaon said. "Saly always refused to talk to Miss Israel or be close to her, but Miss Israel was always trying to get hold of her on different occasions and all the time. Should someone pull out of the competition, it should be Miss Israel."

Miss Israel, Doron Matalon, took to Facebook to express her views.

"It doesn't surprise me, but it still makes me sad," she wrote. "Too bad you cannot put the hostility out of the game, only for three weeks of an experience of a lifetime that we can meet girls from around the world and also from the neighbouring country."

The authorities in Lebanon promised to launch an investigation into the incident and, two days later, gave their blessing for Saly to continue in the pageant.

A beauty queen representing Taiwan in the 2015 Miss Earth pageant proved far less accommodating than her Miss World and Miss Universe peer group who had agreed to change their titles to please the Chinese government.

Ting Wen-yin had been warned before she made her way to Vienna for the final that she could face political pressure from China to swap her Taiwan ROC sash for Chinese Taipei.

But the defiant beauty queen refused, writing on her Facebook page, "I told them 30,000 times that Taiwan is Taiwan. I was born in Taiwan, my sash now says Taiwan, I represent Taiwan, and I'm going to use the name of Taiwan in appearing at this pageant. Their response to me was, 'Change your sash or just leave'."

Ting chose to leave.

The might of China also meant that, at the 2015 Miss World pageant, the Canadian contestant was banned from the final for the first time in its history.

Actress Anastasia Lim was born in China, but moved to Canada with her mother in 2003 at the age of 13, while her father remained in their homeland.

Upon winning the Miss Canada crown, Anastasia used her new title to speak out about her opposition to China's human rights abuses. A staunch defender and practitioner of Falun Gong, a spiritual faith group regarded as an 'evil cult' by the Chinese government and outlawed in 1999, she spoke to a US Congressional committee on the subject of religious persecution two months after winning the pageant in May.

Shortly after she had won Miss Canada, Anastasia's father was visited at home by Chinese security forces, who warned him of the consequences of his daughter continuing to speak out on human rights.

"Dad's really scared," she told the Canadian press. "He doesn't dare talk to me in case his phone is tapped. He doesn't speak his mind anymore. When I pushed him for more details, he just pleaded that I allow him to live peacefully by not bringing up rights abuses in China again. During our brief phone calls now, he always mentions how great the Chinese president, Xi Jinping, is. I think he believes his phone is being tapped."

"I'm not speaking without fear," she added. "I've seen the repercussions."

Despite receiving the backing of the Canadian government for her activism, Anastasia said she had felt ostracised by certain factions of the Canadian-Chinese community, and believed she was being 'monitored' by the Chinese consulate when attending the few community events she was still invited to.

There was always the fear that China – set to host the Miss World final for the sixth time – would not permit her to compete, and those fears were realised just days before the start of the three-week event.

All contestants would receive letters from the Chinese government inviting them to apply for an entry visa, yet Anastasia's letter didn't materialise and the deadline for registering as a finalist in China passed without any word from either the Chinese government, or the Miss World organisation.

"Miss World's line is that if I don't make it to the opening ceremony on 23rd November, I probably can't enter," she told the BBC just three days before that deadline loomed.

Canadian newspaper *The Globe & Mail* contacted the Chinese embassy in Ottawa, to allegedly have been told, "China does not allow any *persona non grata* to come to China."

Yet she was determined that she wouldn't be silenced. "I'm alone and don't even have any family around me, so it's very difficult. Miss World is an international organisation, and if organisations like this don't speak up against the bullying of their own contestants it will continue. China knows it works and they'll just use it again and again until someone stands up to them."

Under Chinese law, citizens from certain countries – including Canada – are eligible for a landing visa upon arrival in China so, on 26th November, she set off for Sanya via Hong Kong.

However, while awaiting her connecting flight in Hong Kong, Anastasia tweeted that she had received a call from a Chinese official telling her not to get on the aircraft as she would not be granted a visa upon arrival.

She later made a statement on her Facebook page, adding that, "Unfortunately, I was prevented from boarding the plane from Hong Kong to Sanya. No reason was given for the denial. The slogan of the Miss World competition is: 'Beauty with a purpose'. My purpose is to advocate for those who cannot speak for themselves – those who suffer in prisons and labor camps, or whose voices have been stifled by repression and censorship."

The pageant continued without her, and Anastasia became the first Miss Canada to fail to compete in Miss World since the national contest began in 1957.

She was invited back to the pageant a year a later by Julia Morley to represent Canada in the final in Washington DC. Some US media organisations complained that the Miss World organisation, with its

Chinese corporate sponsorship, prevented them from speaking to her, but she was granted an interview with the Press Association where she spoke out about her cause.

"Everybody is tied up economically with China," she said. "China's power is so huge that no-one really dares to speak up."

Anastasia failed to make the Top 20 at the pageant, but for her the victory was in the recognition. "The Miss World final is watched by a billion people across the world, and it is broadcast in China," she said. "I have travelled a long journey to get here and I wanted the people to see me on that show."

Pageants and politics will always, it seems, be inextricably linked, despite the beauty queen's clichéd wish for world peace.

"We live in a world full of atrocities, wars, injustice and occupation," said Miss Lebanon 2002, Christine Sawaya, "and seen under that perspective a beauty queen has to understand and respect her country's laws and political positions.

"While it is easy to say forget politics, it is just beauty, it's just a pageant – unfortunately we who live here know that everything is political when it comes to your country's sovereignty and borders."

Ann Sidney, Miss World 1964

I realised I'd become an instant pariah with Julia Morley"

"**G**ood morning, Miss World office. Katie speaking."

"Hello, Katie, this is Ann Sidney. Could I speak to Mrs Morley, please?"

The pause on the other end of the line was but a mere tenth of a second, but long enough to indicate to Ann that her call hadn't been expected – nor that it was particularly welcome.

Katie finally spoke. "I'm sorry, Mrs Morley is in a meeting at the moment. Can I leave a message for her?"

"In actual fact, you may be able to help me," said Ann. "It's fifty years since I won Miss World, and with the pageant being back in London this time, I wondered if I could come and help celebrate my anniversary with you all at the contest?"

This time, there was no mistaking the pause.

"Oh - did you not receive our email?" Katie asked in measured but slightly flustered tones. "Yes, we sent it at least six weeks ago, and never heard back from you. We just presumed you weren't interested?"

Ann was baffled. "Well, no – no, I didn't. I check my email regularly and I've not received anything from you. I've always received your emails in the past and you have all my London and LA phone numbers on file. Which address did you send it to?"

"Ah – ah….I'm not actually at my computer at the moment," Katie floundered. "But – ".

"Well, look," interrupted Ann, "I will email you now, so you have my correct email address, and perhaps you'd be good enough to forward the original to me again. I'll reply immediately, Katie - I'd love to attend."

Katie, having been put very much in the hot seat, replied, "I'll get Julia to call you back as soon as she is out of her meeting."

"Oh, that would be great!" Ann twittered. "I've always supported the Miss World contest throughout the years, and it would be a wonderful memory for me to celebrate my win fifty years ago," adding - laying the flattery on with a trowel - "It truly changed my life!"

Ann put the phone down with a small smile to herself. She felt quite sure that there had been no email that had suddenly got lost in cyberspace and now, by specifically requesting them to send it to her again, she was very firmly putting the cat amongst the pigeons.

Mrs Morley, of course, had many choices among the past Miss Worlds as to whom to invite again, and she clearly had her favourites, Ann realised. She was quite obviously not on that list (and probably, she thought wryly, not even on the reserves list!).

But she wasn't willing to leave it there; 2014 was an important anniversary for her – especially as a home grown winner - and here she was, willing to give her time for free, with no travel or accommodation expenses needing to be paid. Her victory back in 1964 had made a big contribution to the publicity and success of the Miss World organisation and a small recognition was, she felt, a fitting demonstration of their appreciation (and of course a real treat for the pageant fans).

As expected, Ann heard nothing more from the Miss World office.

So how had it come to this? How had it happened that Britain's most celebrated Miss World, the beautiful teenager from Poole who had taken the crown back in 1964 and who had gone on to forge a successful stage career, was not being invited to commemorate the

50th anniversary of her win, in a pageant held in the very town in which she took the title?

Could the reason for the snub conceivably have been due to the presence at the pageant of one of the country's most enduring and popular TV personalities, who would take one look at this stunning beauty queen and decide that it wasn't, to call upon one of his best-known catchphrases, nice to see her, to see her, nice?

Ann certainly had her suspicions that her new *persona non grata* status was down to the Miss World organisation wishing to keep a certain Bruce – later Sir – Forsyth, sweet and on-side.

To understand how we got to this point, let us rewind to 1964, when Ann was crowned Miss World, thus becoming the first of an astonishing three women from Dorset to win the title.

Ann was an apprentice hairdresser when she began her quick rise to success on the beauty circuit. In those days, with the audience ratings in the UK alone at over 23 million at its peak, becoming Miss World was on a par to today's teenagers winning a TV reality show in front of a worldwide audience. Winners became genuine celebrities and for Ann the journey from her modest home in Poole to the bright lights of worldly fame, at the age of just 19, was a heady one.

Ann first met Bruce Forsyth – then aged 35 - just after she had been crowned Miss Front Page in Bournemouth, and while he was starring in a summer season at the Winter Gardens. He was married at the time, but told Ann he was going through a separation from his wife Penny.

Initially, Ann rebuffed Bruce's attentions and romantic overtures. Overwhelmed and feeling out of her depth, she quit her job and, on a whim, took a train to Blackpool in a bid to fulfil her dream of winning the Miss United Kingdom contest.

"Ironically," remarked Ann, "it was Bruce's relentless pursuit of me that proved the catalyst for my taking this risk. You could say that without Bruce I may never have become Miss World!"

Three weeks later she was crowned Miss United Kingdom. The publicity Ann received as a result got a massive boost when, apparently throwing discretion to the wind, Bruce turned up to meet her, champagne in hand, when she flew back to Bournemouth airport the very next day.

Such a rash act kick-started a chain of events that very nearly scuppered her chances at the Miss World contest. Bruce continued in his hot pursuit and, three months later, having separated from his wife, Ann's defences finally came down. Just a week before she was due to join the 43 other contestants for the start of the build-up to the Miss World pageant, Ann allowed herself to fall head over heels for Bruce's sophisticated, witty charms - and that night he laughed her willingly and lovingly into bed.

"I was carrying a big secret when I was crowned Miss World and one that I wasn't particularly proud of," said Ann. "Over the moon with all the attention that I was getting, I foolishly allowed myself to begin an affair with one of the most famous men in Britain."

They were desperate to keep their relationship a secret - "It would've been a scandal in those more conservative times if the press had found out," Ann recalls. But the rumours refused to die down, and the pressure on both he and Ann was immense.

It was Bruce's refusal to make a commitment to her, along with her own guilt over his children and broken marriage, which fuelled the tensions that led to the end of their relationship at the beginning of 1966.

After working for a few years in theatre in England, Ann moved to Los Angeles to pursue a career as a dancer and actress, while Bruce went on famously to marry Miss World 1975, the stunningly beautiful Wilnelia Merced, from Puerto Rico – who, at 23, was thirty years his junior at the time of their wedding in 1983.

Three years earlier, Ann had sold her life story to the *Daily Mirror*, which ran over two days. Bruce was incandescent that one of the days featured a two-page spread documenting a soupcon of the story of their affair, and following publication, he never spoke to her again. Could it be that Bruce had carried a grudge for all those years, and one that he was not prepared to let go of?

"I was very young and inexperienced when I met Bruce at the age of 19," Ann said. "And considering he had written about me in his autobiography a few years later, I thought his attitude was rather contrary."

Bruce had always been a friend and supporter of Eric and Julia Morley's, via not just the Miss World pageant but with their mutual work with the Variety Club of Great Britain. But his association with Miss World didn't extend to any reunion with his former Miss World old flame — not if he could help it, anyway.

It wasn't immediate to Ann that the Miss World organisation had any problem with her. She had, after all, been involved in several reunions of past winners, and been asked to judge the final on a number of occasions — with expenses for economy flights and hotels to the finals in China covered (although there was never a fee involved on any of those judging occasions). It was only when the Miss World bandwagon rolled into London in 2011 that Ann got a taste of the developing *froideur* directed at her from Julia Morley.

Julia had emailed Ann to invite her to attend the 2011 pageant, to be held in London's Earls Court.

"It probably only clicked with the powers that be after I'd accepted that their special guest that night would be Bruce Forsyth," said Ann.

To get Bruce and his wife Wilnelia on stage at Miss World would be a coup; his star was currently shining brighter than ever as host of the BBC's immensely popular *Strictly Come Dancing* show (adapted from the original *Come Dancing* programme devised by none other than Eric Morley).

As a result, Ann was put on the back burner. Despite being asked to keep herself available for the week before the pageant in order to attend functions, she heard nothing from the Miss World office. It was only when she read that Bruce had been present at one of the dinners laid on for contestants that the lightbulb in her mind switched on, and all became clear.

She was finally summonsed to Earls Court the night before the last dress rehearsal, one day before the live final, and assumed she was being invited to judge. Wrong. While the other past winners took their places on the judging panel, Ann suffered the ignominy of being asked to sit, alone, in the auditorium. It was some time before Julia's son Steve Douglas shuffled over to explain to her that she was going to be used for some backstage interviews during the pageant itself, implying that her services were not required until then.

Shrugging off what she perceived to be a snub, Ann returned to her flat in London. A few hours later, she received an email from the director of the show. They were having problems with the length of the broadcast, he said, and as a result they would be seating Ann among the audience in the auditorium, with no guarantee that they would get to her for any of the on-air interviews, or coverage, that Steve Douglas had mentioned earlier.

"I'm not completely daft," said Ann. "I realised that I'd either become an instant pariah with Julia Morley, or that Bruce Forsyth still bore a grudge and was petrified of any contact with me.

"I immediately replied to the director saying that as an professional actress and fully paid up member of Equity, and because this was a live to air show, could he possibly tell me what he required of me: backstage for interviews, or sitting in a seat in the audience?"

Ann could, she said, sense the panic as soon as she'd hit the Send key. "It's as though he realised that perhaps on a *live to air* show it was not in their best interests to sit me in the audience where I could stir up some trouble.

"I allowed myself a rather wicked daydream of throwing a flour or stink bomb at the stage in an echo of the disruption that occurred in the 1970 Miss World contest or, worse, dashing up onstage and grabbing Bruce's straw-coloured toupee to throw it like a frisbee -

whirling around the stadium for all to see - before it landed neatly back on his head again."

Her email did the trick. In a matter of minutes another email popped up from the director, telling Ann that she would be met and immediately ushered backstage by a Miss World employee the next day.

The next afternoon, dressed to the nines, Ann climbed down the narrows stairs of the coach along with the other ex-Miss Worlds, and was grabbed and instantly whisked backstage – where she stayed for the entire evening. She was unseen by either the audience at Earls Court, or by the viewers at home. None of the footage of her interviews with the contestants was shown. "I began to wonder if there was even film in the cameraman's hand-held camera!" she said, only half-joking.

Ironically, it was only after the pageant that Ann nearly bumped into Bruce Forsyth and Wilnelia – "prompting me to give 'em a twirl like his ex-wife Anthea Redfern on *The Generation Game* and turn on my heel pronto to avoid bumping head-on into them both," said Ann, laughing, "You couldn't make it up!"

At the Coronation Ball, she thought better of going over to ask Sir Forsyth for a selfie, and left early like a latter day Cinderella. There was a reason for her premature departure as, unbeknown to the Miss World office, she was booked to appear on ITV's breakfast show the next morning with the new Miss World, Venezuela's Ivian Sarcos.

The piece proved to be a light-hearted affair. When asked by the presenter what she felt was her best attribute Ann, in frivolous mood, lifted her ankle-booted right foot and declared, "My sexy big toe!" The entire studio collapsed into laughter.

In retrospect, after being so blatantly side-lined in 2011, Ann wondered what on earth had made her think she'd be invited to the pageant again, even if she was celebrating her 50th anniversary. But nor was she prepared to lie down and disappear, as they clearly wished her to.

And so it was that Ann precociously rang the Miss World office that October morning, with less than six weeks to go before the 2014 pageant, to be held at London's vast ExCel centre, to check up on her invitation – or lack of it. Her optimism that there had been a genuine misunderstanding on their part took a blow when speaking to one of her contacts. He had previously worked for the Miss World office, and told her bluntly that they would often use this technique – alleging to have sent emails when they quite patently hadn't.

Ann, married to theatrical producer Duncan Weldon, had at that time decided to finally finish her autobiography, and a journalist friend suggested that this snub from the Miss World office – on top of the original slight three years earlier – could provide invaluable publicity for her forthcoming book.

Ann wasn't keen on this idea. Stories of her affair with Bruce had been cobbled together so often in the past for the gossip columns without her involvement or permission, that she couldn't see what possible good it would do. Indeed, Richard Kay's column for the *Daily Mail* had, only a year earlier, reported on Ann's "nights of passion" with Bruce in a rehashed story to publicise her upcoming autobiography – an article which had hardly helped thaw relations. Therefore, bringing Bruce's name up as a potential reason for being cold-shouldered by Miss World was, she considered, just asking for more trouble.

But journalists will be journalists, and when Ann received a phone call from a press reporter soon afterwards, she became aware that the media had got wind of this new story, and a piece was planned for that weekend's *Daily Mail*, one day before the Miss World pageant.

The day before publication, lawyers acting for the *Daily Mail* had contacted the Miss World office to confirm the story and invite a comment from them. Their response was to deny any such snub and insist that Ann had been invited. Minutes later, Ann was surprised to receive a frantic call on her mobile from a secretary. "You must think we are so rude!" she trilled. "Of course you're invited! We have two tickets for you to sit in the audience."

Taken aback at this sudden *volte-face*, Ann pointed out that due to the very late notice, she would have to see if she could change her plans.

It was, by this time, too late to hold the front page (or rather, page 25) of the *Daily Mail*, and the story appeared in the Sebastian Shakespeare gossip column the next day.

Headed, "Ex-Miss World Ann Sidney 'snubbed to spare Brucie's blushes'", it told of how Ann believed she had been deliberately ignored due to her past relationship with Sir Forsyth and its acrimonious ending.

"Bruce is very important to Miss World," Ann was quoted as saying. "He's been a judge on the show and his wife Wilnelia is a former Miss World as well. I've heard rumours that if I appear he may be embarrassed or offended and refuse any future invitations."

The piece included a handsome photo of Ann and Bruce together at a ball in Bournemouth in the 60s, and another of a swimsuit-clad Ann posing in the sea from the same era.

If Ann was worried about Bruce being offended upon publication of the story, it was nothing compared to the reaction from the Miss World office. Ann had emailed them to accept their – albeit forced – invitation of two tickets, only to receive a reply unequivocal in its displeasure.

"Thank you for your email. We were under the impression due to the article written that you were not coming. Not only was the article inaccurate, it was untruthful and we feel deeply offended that this was alleged. We had no part whatsoever in your decision-making not to come."

It was signed "Mr A Jones".

And so the 2014 Miss World pageant proceeded without Ann's presence, or any acknowledgement whatsoever of her win fifty years previously.

She knew she would never be invited nor contacted by the Miss World organisation again, but feels no bitterness towards them.

"I feel both the 2011 and 2014 episodes were badly managed," Ann said, "and quite frankly their attitude towards me has ensured that I am not in the slightest bit upset that I will no longer be involved. I will always support the contest and wish the winners well, though, and will always acknowledge how winning the crown has shaped my life."

When Sir Bruce died in August 2017 following a long illness, Ann expressed condolences to his widow Wilnelia and his family on her Facebook page. She also gave an interview to the *Mail on Sunday* about her relationship with Britain's longest-serving entertainer and to pay tribute to the man whom she adored to the very end.

"He was a wonderful man who helped shape and change my life," she said. "And what a life he had. I shall forever be grateful for his love, and I shall never forget him."

Ann's final contact with the Miss World organisation was to reply to Mr A Jones, once more requesting a copy of the original email they had allegedly sent her inviting her to the pageant.

She's still waiting.

With my very special thanks to Ann Sidney for talking to me so openly and honestly about her experiences, and for her kind permission to include this story in my book. Ann's own autobiography, Surviving Miss World, chronicling her extraordinary life and experiences before, during and after the Miss World pageant, will be published shortly.

Tommy Cooper's Beauty Queens in Dentures

Memories of the judging panel by Jon Osborne
Former Director of Miss World Ltd

I have the Miss World organisation to thank for the day I was phoned by the *News of the World* to ask me to provide an obituary for Lord Laurence Olivier.

The legendary actor was very ill and not expected to recover, and the researcher on the other end of the line was requesting my input in preparation for his demise. It was only after a brief, confusing conversation that I realised that the caller was after that other, rather more high-profile, John (with an 'h') Osborne, the celebrated playwright who wrote the classic *Look Back In Anger*.

The confusion came about because, several years earlier, I had sold my story of backstage at the Miss World pageant to the *News of the World*, and was on their list of contacts as an 'informant' for other titbits I may have about the contest (including the exclusive that the BBC were axing their coverage of the Miss England pageant). So when the researcher looked in his file under "Osborne, J" he mistakenly rang me instead of that other, rather angrier, young man.

My upbringing in the one traffic light town of Pageland, South Carolina – with a population of 1,500 – could have hampered my chances of rubbing shoulders with the calibre of celebrities I came to meet and know during my career. But I was fortunate to have a passion for film and theatre, an obsession stoked nicely by the two cinemas in the town.

It was this love of stagecraft and glamour that led me, in later years, to produce the Watermelon Queen pageant. The Pageland Watermelon Festival – held annually to celebrate the town's number one crop - was the biggest date in the town's calendar, bringing in thousands of visitors, and the Watermelon Queen pageant was second only to Miss South Carolina in the number of contestants it attracted. The guest of honour at the event was the reigning Miss America who, in those days, was the equivalent to royalty in the States.

During one year's Festival, I produced the pageant that crowned not only the Watermelon Queen, but South Carolina's representative to the Miss World USA contest, the winner of whom would fly to London for the Miss World final. Obtaining that franchise was the passport I needed to a world of eminent people and celebrities, and led to my first meeting with Julia Morley in London.

Mrs Morley hired me to join the staff of Mecca Promotions and I eventually became a Director of Miss World Limited.

A year earlier, on a previous trip to London, I met Julia Morley's nephew Ed Crozier, who invited me to sit in the audience of Miss World 1969 – not only my first Miss World, but the first held in the Royal Albert Hall. Eva Reuber-Staier took the crown for Austria, while the runner-up – Gail Renshaw of the USA – was not-so-secretly having an affair with singing heartthrob Dean Martin, to whom she was briefly engaged after the pageant.

Having not moved to London until 1970 I, to my woeful regret, missed the Swinging Sixties. Being a staunch fan of The Beatles, I was amused to hear Eric Morley tell the judges of Miss UK 1977 that it was he who had discovered them. Seemingly, the band would've had no career whatsoever if Eric hadn't booked them to play a Mecca venue in Liverpool! The judges feigned suitable admiration for Eric's alleged contribution to the music industry.

Had I been born a decade earlier and started working at Miss World then, I'd have been around to see Bob Hope crown Rosemarie Frankland as Miss World 1961, and witness the start of a long-term affair between them. I'd have seen Catharina Lodders win Miss World 1962 and go on to marry singing legend Chubby Checkers.

I'd also have met America's Diana Batts, runner up to Miss World 1965, who changed her name professionally to Dian Parkinson and appeared from 1975 to 1993 as a hostess on *The Price Is Right* in the States. A year after her departure from the show, she filed a lawsuit against Bob Barker for sexual harassment, claiming a three-year sexual relationship was extorted by threats of firing her from the TV show. The suit was withdrawn in April 1995, Diana claiming it was too costly and had taken a toll on her health. Bob Barker was familiar to pageant viewers as the television host for Miss Universe pageants for many years.

My fantasy 1960s re-birth would also have allowed me to see the stunning Shakira Baksh finish second runner-up in Miss World 1967, representing Guyana. She may have lost Miss World, but was to gain a far more important title – that of Lady. The legendary actor Michael Caine became obsessed with Shakira after seeing her in a TV advert for Maxwell House coffee and, after discovering she lived only a few miles from him in London, set about wooing her. They married in 1973 and Caine was knighted by the Queen in 2000.

My 'real life' at Miss World began in 1970, one of the most controversial years in the pageant's history – and my first opportunity to meet some proper celebrities at last!

At my first Miss World, I came face to face with judges Douglas Fairbanks Jnr, Glen Campbell, Joan Collins and one who probably in hindsight wished he had stayed away - Sir Eric Gairy, the Prime Minister of Grenada. Sir Gairy's island country in the Caribbean had never participated in an international beauty contest before. However, Julia Morley's secretary Susan Dixon had lived in Grenada for a period of time before joining Mecca Promotions and due to her contacts, Grenada agreed to send a representative and their Prime Minister agreed to judge.

That panel, like so many others, had no understanding of the rather complicated process used to name the winner. Eric Morley had adopted the Skating System which was used for ballroom dance championships. With the Skating System and nine judges (the usual make-up of a Miss World panel), a contestant could receive four firsts but lose. If no contestant acquired the majority (at least five first place votes), second and third placings came into play. As it happened, in 1970 the winner had only two first places but all other judges had her at least second or third. And Miss Sweden with four firsts fell to fourth place because the remaining five judges didn't give her any seconds or thirds. Confused? You're not alone. The Skating System, which Morley swore was the fairest, was truly only fully understood by him and the adjudicator, who was the Editor of *Dance News*, the Bible of the Ballroom Dance community.

Because of the difficulty in grasping the Skating System, many cried foul when Miss Grenada took the title. Her Prime Minister may have been pleased that his country won on their first try but he didn't take pleasure in being a part of the "fix" rumours. I may have been introduced to some people of renown during my first year, but I was also introduced to an element of Miss World that brought most of the press coverage - controversy. 1970 was controversial not only for those who questioned the choice, but also for the havoc created during the live broadcast.

Bob Hope was featured in the show - chalking up another major celeb I got to meet! He was delivering his monologue to the Royal Albert Hall audience when disruptors began making a great deal of noise and started throwing smoke bombs onto the stage, an incident memorialised in volume one of *Misdemeanours*.

As an American abroad, it had been an honour to meet Mr Hope just prior to his appearance on the programme. However, it was disappointing to see this man - seen as a hero for going into war zones to entertain troops overseas - fleeing the stage in utter panic as soon as the commotion began. Julia Morley grabbed him as he exited and sent him back on stage to gain control of the crowd as security removed the agitators, who turned out to be members of the Women's Liberation Movement. Even more disappointing was when he surmised, in his attempt to calm the situation, that the perpetrators must have been "on some sort of dope."

Mecca Promotions organised other televised events including *Miss England, Miss Scotland, Miss Wales, Miss United Kingdom*, and *Come*

Dancing, which became one of the longest running television series of all time. *Come Dancing* morphed into *Strictly Come Dancing* in the UK and *Dancing With The Stars* in America, as well as being sold all round the world.

During my entire time with Miss World, I was the one responsible for coordinating *Come Dancing* and one of my tasks was obtaining a guest judge for the panel that awarded points to the freestyle presentations. I finally got to meet the fabulous Ann Sidney, Miss World 1964, when she was guest judge at a venue in Bournemouth.

During my years dealing with beauty queens, I never witnessed any really mean, bitchy rivalry between them. Ballroom dancers were the real divas. But while many of the dancers may have been difficult, the host of *Come Dancing* was anything but. The late, great Terry Wogan was the nicest, wittiest celebrity I ever met and worked with. What joy to be backstage or in the Green Room with him! Terry also hosted many of Mecca's beauty pageants on the BBC for a number of years and was never anything but the consummate professional.

We also staged other competitions that did not receive telly coverage like the Efferdent Winning Smile contest (at which one of the judges Tommy Cooper, comedian and magician, got upset when he realised he was assessing the smiles of contestants wearing dentures!), Jersey Holiday Queen, Miss Britain, Miss Lovely Legs, and Miss Top Teen.

When Miss Top Teen was held at London's Lyceum Theatre, the sponsor had been promised a panel of prominent personalities as the judges. We had obtained several who were names in the business but no one major. My nemesis at the office was Julia's sister who frantically tried to talk agents into letting one of their clients be a judge. Me, well I got on the phone to a fellow American I had met socially at a pub one Sunday afternoon and he turned out to be the right hand man to *The Man From U.N.C.L.E.* Robert Vaughn who was living in Victoria while shooting a movie in London. The right hand man came through for me and I was able to announce that Vaughn was prepared to judge! My nemesis was defeated - she couldn't top Vaughn - but it would take her another nine years to get her revenge and engineer my leaving Miss World.

Another judge was actor Peter Denyer, from popular TV show *Please Sir*. We became friends and when I needed to move closer to my work, he offered me a place in his large top floor flat in Bayswater together with four others. The fifth person living with us at Moscow Road was a non-celeb like me but he was the most revered due to his connections that kept us supplied with an array of drugs.

Jimmy Armstrong was a young Glasgow lad who had a stall in the Portobello Market. He was quite a charmer and was able to bed two of the Miss Worlds I brought back to our place – one being the 1972 winner from Australia, Belinda Green, who had been a clear favourite with the judges which included David Bailey and Peter Sellers.

To the hard working waiting staff at the Albert Hall who served lunch and snacks to the contestants and crew once rehearsals got underway, all of these beauties were celebrities. They tried ever so hard to communicate with the girls so they could go home at night and tell their families they had waited on Miss This or Miss That.

Their congenial attitude toward the competitors gave me one of my all-time favourite Miss World stories. In 1972 the drive was on to achieve participation from 60 countries, due to the fact that the Miss Universe pageant held earlier that year had had a record 61 entered. Therefore, when we were approached by a local businessman in London who said he could produce a Miss Hong Kong for us, we jumped at his proposal and were prepared to overlook how she was being chosen to represent her country.

A tall young woman with a rather muscular frame arrived to register as Miss Hong Kong at the Britannia Hotel in our Admin Office. She had the provocative name of Mei-Lin Gay and the chaperones swore she was a fellow. I saw her passport and could attest that she was not - unless the document had been altered in some way.

More perplexing though was her accent. English is one of the two main languages spoken in Hong Kong but Mei-Lin's accent had no hint of any Asian influence: it was pure Cockney.

One day during a lunch break at the Albert Hall, she was seated with several of the other reps from Asia including Miss Japan and Miss Korea, neither of whom spoke much English, although their chaperones were also at the table to help them converse. A sweet little British lady came to take their orders and proceeded to make friendly chat with Miss Japan. Her chaperone explained Miss Japan spoke very limited English but might be able to understand a word or two if the waitress asked slowly and, if not, she would interpret. The waitress addressed Miss Japan and enquired, "How long, luv, did it take you to get here?" Miss Japan nodded sweetly and the chaperones put the question to her so that Miss Japan could respond.

The waitress then turned to Mei-Lin and ever so slowly but loudly this time asked,
"AND...YOU...LUV...HOW...LONG...DID...IT...TAKE...YOU...TO...GET...HERE?" Without hesitation, Mei-Lin replied, "About 15 minutes on a number 9 bus." The waitress was amazed she had conversed so well with a foreigner and the chaperone – desperately trying not to laugh - couldn't wait to relay this moment to us all. Amid much hilarity, we wondered if Mei-Lin had ever actually set foot in Hong Kong at all!

Miss World 1973 hit the jackpot in terms of celebrity judges, with Gregory Peck, Michael Crawford, Englebert Humperdinck and Christopher Lee all gracing the panel. It is not without irony that Peck, who had won the Best Actor Oscar for his role as a lawyer in *To Kill A Mockingbird* – "a paragon of honour and virtue" – should help choose the USA's Marji Wallace as winner, who was sacked four months later for her alleged lack of honour and virtue and all round moral turpitude!

Earlier that year I had a brush with celebrity that remains the one memory I would most like to have erased from my mind and one that years later would mean I had been awfully close to an involvement with someone who came to define moral turpitude as an inherent quality of baseness, vileness, or depravity.

At the final for Miss Top Teen held at the Lyceum, the judge who caused me this distress was Paul Francis Gadd. Well, that was his birth name. On the road to success in the music industry, he had the monikers of Paul Raven and, no kidding, Rubber Bucket. By the time he judged he was very popular for his extreme glam image of glitter suits, make-up, platform boots and his energetic performances as Gary Glitter. After Miss Top Teen had been crowned, I got a message in the Green Room that the limo we had hired to take Glitter home had arrived and had parked near the stage entrance.

I informed Glitter that his ride awaited and escorted him to the stage entrance at the back of the Lyceum, onto the darkened street and over to the limo. As I went to open the car door for him, he swung me around and pinned me to the car, pulled me close and planted a kiss on my mouth which he tried to ply open with his tongue as he groped me. I pushed him away and stopped short of spitting out his taste as he climbed into the back seat laughing off the incident as the limo drove away.

This guy who had 21 hit singles and was among the Top 100 most successful chart acts in the UK (including at the time of my encounter the eerily apt *Do You Wanna Touch Me*) would become better known by the public nearly 30 years later for being sentenced to prison for possession of child pornography, child sexual abuse and attempted rape. Given my own experience of being violated by him, I wasn't surprised to read of his downfall.

Acts of moral turpitude waiting to be revealed played a major role in the choice of Miss United Kingdom 1974. Joining judges including Michael Parkinson and Nerys Hughes – who had no idea that they would be picking the one contestant whose virtue would be a subject of debate and controversy for months to come – was one Jimmy Savile.

Savile, host of TV's *Jim'll Fix It*, was a friend of Eric Morley's through their days working the clubs and their commitments to Variety Club children's charities. Over the course of his lifetime, Savile was estimated to have raised over £40m for charity, as well as establishing himself as a friend of the Royal Family and a national treasure.

When host David Vine spoke to Savile during the broadcast of Miss UK, Savile said, "I am the best-qualified person to judge this beauty contest, being asexual and having no interest in sex whatsoever."

Those words appeared desperately hollow when, after his death in 2011, Scotland Yard launched Operation Yewtree, an investigation into allegations of child abuse by the star – who was knighted in 1990 - spanning six decades. The scandal resulted in inquiries at the BBC, NHS and Crown Prosecution Service, with Savile said to have abused more than 1,000 victims, aged between 5 and 75. A combination of his celebrity status and influence, and police errors, allowed him to escape detection until after his death.

So when Savile voted for Helen Morgan to become Miss United Kingdom, he had no knowledge that she would face a challenge to her morals within days of the crowning, while the audience and contestants had no inkling that Savile would one day be at the centre of one of the biggest scandals ever to taint the entertainment industry.

As reported in the first volume of *Misdemeanours*, Helen did not resign as Miss World because it was discovered she had a child out of wedlock. That discovery came within one day of her victory as Miss United Kingdom, when Helen informed us at Mecca Promotions that she had a son. Julia Morley made the decision to let Helen retain her title and compete for Miss World, a decision accepted quite well by the British public but not so much by the overseas franchise holders for Miss World. They felt that the Morleys were being hypercritical in allowing Helen to compete, having sacked the previous winner for her dubious morals.

Especially upset was the American franchise holder - who had seen his winner dethroned the year before – and all of the franchise holders for the South American countries who took pride in sending 'good' girls with Catholic moral values to compete.

Helen stepped down as Miss World when the paternity of her son was going to be the focus of a *Daily Mirror* investigation. The same paper also got the tip-off to be on hand to whisk Helen away to go into hiding while her resignation was front page news. I learned of Helen's decision when Julia called me at home to ask Belinda Green (Miss World 1972) to take over appearances for Helen until runner-up Anneline Kriel was awarded the title.

Shortly beforehand a flatmate, Peter Firth, had left to star in a play on Broadway, so I offered the spare rooms to Belinda and her friend Paula Whitehead, Miss Australia in the 1972 Miss International pageant, for a six month stay in London.

We were soon joined by actor Leon Vitale and his girlfriend, who slept on giant beanbags while they found a flat of their own. One night the phone rang in the flat. Paula answered it and we watched as she fainted to the floor. It was only when Vitale retrieved the handset that he realised why she had reacted in this way – the voice on the other end of the phone was none other than his friend Ryan O'Neal, with whom he was currently filming.

The shock of actually speaking to the biggest superstar of the era had been too much for the poor girl!

Donald Trump, President of the United States of America

"I'm standing backstage with these women with no clothes and I get away with it."

When the subject of a book is supposed to be about female beauty queens, it takes a very rare species of man to star in no less than three chapters of his own.

But, whatever your political persuasion, few would disagree that Donald Trump – who pulled off one of the biggest shocks in election history to become the 45th President of the United States of America – is no ordinary man.

Trump's starring role in the *Misdemeanours* series began in Volume 1, long before he revealed any political ambition. Back then, he was merely President of The Trump Organisation, owner of the Miss Universe, Miss USA and Miss Teen USA pageants, and a TV celebrity, courtesy of *The Apprentice* business game show.

Volume 1 told the story of Trump's very public humiliation of his 1996 Miss Universe winner, Alicia Machado, who piled on the pounds during her reign to such an alarming degree that he castigated her on national television and made her take exercise in front of photographers.

The full story of Trump's resurrection of the Miss Universe brand, and his fall from grace following racists remarks as he launched his bid for the US Presidency, was recounted in *More Misdemeanours*, while another chapter told of his role in the controversy of a transgender Miss Canada contestant.

Not content with this trio of tales, Trump was featured heavily in Carrie Prejean's story, during which he sacked her as Miss California USA for breach of contract.

So it is no surprise that the man himself makes yet more appearances within the pages of Volume 3. And, for that once-overweight Miss Universe from Venezuela, who had been waiting years for this moment, revenge was not only a dish best served cold, but the sweetest taste of all.

Trump must have hoped that his spat with Alicia Machado had long since been forgotten, yet he failed to realise that, when you're standing as the Republican nomination for President of the United States of America - and when your opponent is Hillary Clinton - not a single misdemeanour is ever allowed to die.

The moment Trump and Clinton were anointed as the two candidates to stand in the election to choose the 45th President, the gloves were off between them, with the backroom staff of both teams forensically searching night and day for the smallest shred of evidence with which to wound and destroy the other.

Clinton chose to play one of her Trump cards very early on, during the first of three televised debates between the two nominees on 26th September, after Trump accused her of "not having a presidential look."

"This," Clinton announced to the packed auditorium, "is a man who has called women pigs, slobs and dogs. Who has said women don't deserve equal pay unless they do as good a job as men. And one of the worst things he said was about a woman in a beauty contest - he loves beauty contests, supporting them and hanging around them - and he called this woman 'Miss Piggy'. Then he called her 'Miss Housekeeping' because she was Latina."

Fixing a steely and knowing look at her rival, she continued, "Donald, she has a name. Her name - ."

"Where did you find this?" Trump interjected. "Where did you find this?"

" - is Alicia Machado," Clinton continued. "And she has become a US citizen. And you can bet she's going to vote this November."

As the audience burst into applause, the Clinton camp would have been forgiven for performing a round of high fives. By mentioning the subject of female appearance, Trump had quite beautifully given Clinton the opportunity to resurrect the story from 20 years earlier, one that her team had lined up for her during their methodical research.

The media called it Clinton's "best moment" of the debate, and that perfectly-timed killer response was shown on news summaries across the world. Social media asked, "Who is Alicia Machado?", giving the press *cart blanche* to remind readers of the story of Trump's first winner after his takeover of the Miss Universe organisation in 1996.

Alicia herself basked in the attention and grabbed at the opportunity to finally see her former puppet-master having to eat humble pie over her treatment at his hands two decades ago. In a video produced by the Clinton campaign and released after the debate, Alicia told of her impressions of Trump.

"He was overwhelming," she said. "I was very scared of him. He'd tell me, 'You look ugly', or 'You look fat'. Sometimes he would 'play' with me and say, 'Hello Miss Piggy', 'Hello Miss Housekeeping.'

"I earned the Miss Universe organisation a lot of money. By contract, I should've earned 10% on all the commercials and work I did. I was never paid."

The video went on to explain that during her reign as Miss Universe, she gained weight. Trump threatened to take her title away and invited reporters to watch her working out. The video showed a clip of Trump telling a reporter, "She weighed 118 or 117 pounds and she went up to 160 or 170. So this is somebody who likes to eat."

Over footage from 1996 of Alicia exercising on machines in front of a bank of cameramen, she said, "It was very humiliating. I felt really bad, like a lab rat. It had turned into a circus, the joke of The Fat Miss Universe. A joke that caused me a lot of pain."

Alicia said that after her reign was over she was sick with eating disorders. "I wouldn't eat - I would still see myself as fat, because a powerful man had said so. This is a man who doesn't realise the damage he causes. He bears many grudges and harbours a deep racism.

"But now I am strong. I am an American citizen - and I am going to vote. That's why I dare speak about all this. Donald Trump lacks the experience, preparation and human qualities to be president of the United States."

The video ended with the words, "Donate today at hillaryclinton.com".

The New York Times estimated that, in the 48 hours following the debate, Alicia's publicity blitz had resulted in her being mentioned over 200,000 times on Twitter, and referred to on American TV over 6,000 times, with political commentators concluding that the story presented a 'golden opportunity' for Clinton to reach the Hispanic community in key battleground states.

Yet Trump wasn't about to accept what he considered to be a 'public smear campaign' against him without attacking back. Within hours of the story breaking, the media was reporting that in the early 1990s, Alicia was accused of abetting an attempted murder committed by her then-boyfriend after he shot a relative in Carcacas. Alicia was reportedly seen driving the getaway car, but she did not face charges. She also denied threatening the Venezuelan judge who presided over the case.

Furthermore, she was questioned about a 1997 interview in which she had said she had suffered from anorexia before the Miss Universe pageant. Alicia denied saying this, despite the original clip still being widely available.

Trump himself could hardly deny Alicia's fat-shaming story, having orchestrated the press coverage at the time himself, but wasn't about to take the attack lying down. At an hour when he *should've* been lying down - 3am - he tweeted a series of messages about her, including, "Did Crooked Hillary help disgusting (check out sex tape and past) Alicia M become a U.S. citizen so she could use her in the debate?"

The sex tape allegation appeared to be false, and referred merely to racy scenes in a Spanish-language reality show that Alicia appeared in in 2005.

For Trump, his "worst ever Miss U" was merely the tip of an iceberg that would result in his entire eligibility to carry on as a presidential candidate being called into question.

Less than two weeks after that televised debate, an audio and video recording from 2005 was published online by *The Washington Post* that would prove to potentially be the final nail in Trump's presidential coffin.

TV anchor Billy Bush – nephew of former President George H W Bush, former co-host of both Miss Universe and Miss USA pageants and, at that time, co-host of the *Today* programme – was overheard during his coverage of the Rio Olympics that he had a tape of "Trump being a real dog". Staff members from the NBC network began a feverish search for the tape and got hold of it but, due to delays for legal clearance and the breaking news from Hurricane Matthew, they were scooped by *The Washington Post.*

The video captured Trump arriving with Billy Bush – then host of the *Access Hollywood* show – arriving by bus onto the set of the *Days of Our Lives* soap opera, in which Trump would film a cameo role.

Trump, who was 59 at the time and newly married to wife Melania, talked about a married woman upon whom he "moved on and failed. I did try and **** her. She was married. I moved on her like a bitch.

"Then all of a sudden I see her, she's now got the big, phoney tits and everything. She's totally changed her look."

At this stage, a laughing Billy Bush spotted *Days of Our Lives* actress Arianna Zucker waiting for them outside the bus.

"Sheesh, your girl's as hot as shit," Bush remarked.

"Look at you, you are a pussy," said Trump. "I better use some Tic Tacs in case I start kissing her. You know I'm automatically attracted to beautiful – I just start kissing them. It's like a magnet. Just kiss. I don't even wait.

"And when you're a star, they let you do it. You can do anything. Grab them by the pussy. You can do anything."

The fall-out from the release of the tape was immediate and – for Trump's presidential hopes – catastrophic. Hillary Clinton tweeted, "This is horrific. We cannot allow this man to be President," while even his hitherto staunch supporters described his words as "inappropriate and offensive" and his actions "amounting to sexual assault."

The tape appeared at the worst possible time for Trump, when he was seeking to make an issue out of his opponent's marriage.

"Hillary Clinton was married to the single greatest abuser in the history of politics," he had recently told *The New York Times*. "Hillary was an enabler, and she attacked the women who Bill Clinton had mistreated."

With his presidential campaign plunged into crisis, Trump initially dismissed his words as "locker room banter, a private conversation that took place many years ago. Bill Clinton has said far worse to me on the golf course, not even close. I apologise if anyone was offended."

As his fellow Republicans - and the Speaker of the House – lined up to condemn him and distance themselves from him, Trump was forced to issue a more sincere apology, and released a 90 second video to the media (yet was still unable to resist mentioning Bill Clinton's physical abuse of women and Hillary's intimidation of her husband's victims).

In response to the controversy, singer Carly Simon donated her 1972 smash hit single *You're So Vain* for use in an anti-Trump TV commercial, while Trump's wife Melania denounced his words as "unacceptable and offensive to me. This does not represent the man I know."

As the storm continued to rage, several dozen Republicans called on Trump to withdraw from the campaign, and allow his running mate Mike Pence to take over in an attempt to repair the damage. But even if it had been legally possible to change the candidacy at this late stage, Trump insisted that he would never stand down.

Entertainment Tonight co-host Nancy O'Dell was revealed as being the married woman at the centre of Trump's crude recording. A former Miss South Carolina and finalist for Miss America and Miss USA, Nancy became a well-known TV anchor in the States and co-hosted the Miss USA and Miss Universe pageants in both 2004 and 2005.

"The conversation needs to change," Nancy said in a statement, "because no female, no person, should be the subject of such crass comments, whether or not the cameras are rolling."

Billy Bush, meanwhile, issued an apology for his part in the damning recording, but never returned to *The Today Show* following the leaking of the tape, and a week later it was announced that he had left his post at NBC, having reached a financial settlement.

Yet Trump's troubles were only just beginning. Days later, half a dozen women came forward to reveal to the press that they had been sexually assaulted by him in ways similar to those he had described gleefully on the recording.

One described how she was "cornered in a lift" by him and "kissed directly on the mouth", while another alleged that he had "hands like an octopus" as she sat next to him on a flight to New York in the early 80s.

But it was the accusations levelled against him by his former beauty queens that really hit home.

Miss Washington USA 2013, Cassandra Searles, shared a photo from the Miss USA pageant on her Facebook page, with the caption, "Do y'all remember that one time we had to do our on-stage introductions, but this one guy treated us like cattle and made us do it all again because we didn't look him in the eye? Do you also remember when he then proceeded to have us all lined up so he could get a closer look at his property? He probably doesn't want me telling the story about that time he continually grabbed my ass and invited me to his hotel room.

"Oh I forgot to tell you that guy will be in the running for the next President of the United States. I love the idea of having a misogynist as President."

Miss Mississippi USA, Paromita Mitra, agreed and replied, "I literally have nightmares about that process."

Several contestants from the Miss Teen USA pageant - where the entrants were as young as 15 - had already accused Trump of leering over them as they changed outfits backstage.

Miss Vermont Teen USA 1997, Mariah Billado, told the *Buzzfeed* website, "I remember putting on my dress really quick, because I was like, oh my God, there's a man in here."

Trump allegedly told them at the time, "Don't worry, ladies, I've seen it all before."

That same year, the reigning Miss Universe, Brooke Lee, recalled Trump asking her opinion of his daughter Ivanka, who was co-hosting the Miss Teen USA pageant. "Don't you think my daughter's hot?" he asked Brooke. "She's hot, right?"

At the Miss USA 1997 pageant, Miss Utah Temple Taggart, revealed that Trump kissed her "directly on my lips. I thought, 'Oh my God, gross'.

And Miss Arizona USA 2001, Tasha Dixon, gave a damning interview to the CBS network revealing how Trump "just came strolling right in" to the changing area. "There was no second to put a robe on, or any sort of clothing or anything. Some girls were topless. Other girls were naked. Our first introduction to him was when we were at the dress rehearsal and half-naked changing into our bikinis."

Tasha went on to say that the employees of the Miss Universe Organisation encouraged the contestants to lavish Trump with attention when he came in. "To have the owner come waltzing in, when we're naked, or half-naked, in a very physically vulnerable position and then to have the pressure of the people that worked for him telling us to go fawn over him, go walk up to him, talk to him, get his attention.

"Who do you complain to?" she asked. "He owns the pageant. There's nobody to complain to. Everyone there works for him."

Trump's staff refused to respond to the stories, but footage of his appearance on *The Howard Stern Show* in 2005 emerged, in which he bragged about doing exactly what the women had described.

"I'll go backstage before a show, and everyone's getting dressed and ready and everything else," he told Stern. "You know, no men are anywhere. And I'm allowed to go in because I'm the owner of the pageant. And therefore I'm inspecting it...Is everyone okay? You know, they're standing there with no clothes. And you see these incredible-looking women. And so I sort of get away with things like that."

In the same interview he refused to say whether he had ever slept with a contestant, before joking that it may be an "obligation" of the job.

Carrie Jean Prejean, sacked as Miss California USA 2009 by Trump for breach of contract, recalled in her memoirs, *Still Standing*, that Trump would force the contestants to rate each other's looks on the spot, a humiliation that would reduce them to tears:

"Donald Trump walked out with his entourage and inspected us closer than any general ever inspected a platoon. He would stop in front of a girl, look her up and down, and say, 'Hmmm'. Then he would go on and do the same thing to the next girl. He took notes on a little pad as he went along."

Carrie went on to say that Trump then called all the women forward and asked each one, "Tell me, who's the most beautiful woman here?"

"It became clear," Carrie continued, "that the whole point of the exercise was for him to divide the room between the girls he personally found attractive and those he did not. Some of the girls were sobbing backstage after he left, devastated to have failed to impress 'The Donald' even before the competition had begun."

Carrie's recollection was confirmed by an audio recording from the same year, obtained by the *TMZ* website, on which Trump could be heard asking the contestants for help in picking out some of the best-looking women before the pageant took place.

"We get to choose a certain number of contestants who will be guaranteed to make it through the first round," he said on the recording. "You know why we do that? Because years ago when I first bought it, we chose ten people, I chose none and I get here and the most beautiful people were not chosen. And I went nuts. So we call it The Trump Rule."

Miss Universe Finland 2006, Ninni Laaksonen, became the 12th woman to come forward and accuse Trump of abuse. Recalling the occasion she appeared with him on *The Late Show* with David Letterman, she said that when they posed for photographers beforehand, "Trump stood next to me and suddenly squeezed my butt. He really grabbed my butt. I don't think anyone saw it but I flinched and thought, 'What is happening?'"

During one of the parties that took place during the build-up to the Miss Universe pageant, Ninni was told that Trump liked her because "I looked like his wife Melania when she was younger. It left me disgusted."

Following such a thorough character assassination, the Trump campaign issued a statement to *Rolling Stone* magazine, denying the beauty queens' allegations and questioning the political motivation behind them, adding, "Mr Trump has a fantastic record of empowering women throughout his career, and a more accurate story would be to show how he's been a positive influence in the lives of so many."

Trump went further when appearing on *Good Morning America*. "The stories are all false," he stated. "All of these liars will be sued once the election is over."

One rare and completely unexpected source of support came from an actual former Miss USA. Chelsea Cooley, who was crowned Miss USA 2004, gave an exclusive interview to the *Daily Mail*, in which she expressed gratitude towards Trump for the kindness and generosity he showed her as her personal business mentor.

"In terms of Donald acting inappropriately towards women, I have never seen him be anything but a consummate gentleman," she said.

"I have known him for eleven years now," she continued, "and when I asked him to be my business mentor, he said, absolutely, I will do whatever I can to help you. He didn't have to, because he gets absolutely nothing out of it."

Of the sexual assault claims, Chelsea questioned their timing. "I am shocked," she said. "Less than a month out from the election, it's all coming out now? You can't help but look at the timing and question it. I have never experienced anything like that with Donald, so why would you bring it up now? Why would you not come out about it before if it happened and if were something that greatly bothered you?"

In what was seen as the ugliest presidential race in history, Trump's name had been tarnished to such a degree by the accusations that any hope of victory seemed irrevocably jeopardised, and Hillary Clinton's narrow lead in the polls began to widen by the largest margin seen in the campaign so far. It was also widely agreed that Hillary was the winner of the third and final televised debate on 20th October.

However, a week is a long time in politics. The revelation that the FBI were re-opening their investigation into emails sent by Hillary on a personal email server in 2009, shortly before she became Secretary of State, gave Trump's camp one final and much-needed boost and, with only seven days to go before the election on 8th November, Hillary's lead in the polls was slashed to just one point.

It was still enough, the polls and the pundits predicted, to give Hillary a win, and very few who chose to stay up to watch the results come in would have considered any other result.

But at 2.40am on Wednesday, 9th November, 2016 - a date and time that will forever be recalled through a fog of surrealism and shock - Donald J Trump swept to victory as the 45th President of the United States of the America. And, just as in his election campaign, his triumph alienated half the population in one fell swoop before he had even opened his mouth to deliver his victory speech.

Trump's inauguration hadn't even taken place before yet more lurid stories from yet more beauty queens rolled. A former Miss Hungary by the name of Kata Sarka alleged that, at a party following the 2013 Miss Universe pageant hosted in Moscow (for which Trump had struck a $20 million deal), he approached her, grabbed her hand, and asked, "Who are you?"

Taken aback, she replied. Trump then handed her his business card and invited her to his hotel room, despite having been married to his wife Melania for eight years at that point.

This story came hot on the heels of an allegation by a British ex-MI6 spy claiming that Russia had 'compromising evidence' with which to blackmail the president-elect. The alleged dossier claims that Trump let prostitutes perform a 'degrading sex act' in a Moscow hotel room during the same Miss Universe pageant, that he used the services of Russian prostitutes, and that he had attended sex parties.

Trump branded the story as "fake news", but the controversy rumbles on.

It remains to be seen whether President Trump will be in the White House long enough to earn a chapter in *Misdemeanours* Volume 4 but, as the great man said himself, "Anyone who thinks my story is anywhere near over is sadly mistaken."

Donald Trump and his Miss Universe nemesis, Alicia Machado

Julia Lemigova, Miss USSR 1991, and her wife
Martina Navratilova

Rana Raslan, crowned the first Arab Miss Israel in 1999

The author with Zara Holland just after her crowning as Miss Great Britain 2015

Rima Fakih, the first Muslim to be crowned Miss USA

The author with Ann Sidney in 2015

Ann Sidney is crowned Miss World 1964

The Miss World organisers deny that the year as Miss World destroys relationships, but they will admit that it can be a head-turning period. 'It depends on the strength of the relationship and on the individual,' says John Osborne.

Jon Osborne speaks to the press in 1975 while working at the Miss World office

Miss Great Britain – 1990-Present

"It was fourteen months of hell"
Liz Fuller, Miss Great Britain director 2009-2011

Following Lancaster City Council's decision to cut ties with the Miss Great Britain pageant after the 1989 winner was crowned, no contests were held between 1990 and 1994 as the iconic brand searched for owners to take it into a new decade.

The next era of the pageant began in 1995, when businessmen John and David Singh bought the Miss Great Britain trademark and offered the franchise to parties interested in running the contest in exchange for a tidy fee.

Miss Great Britain had always been a stand-alone pageant, in that the winner didn't go on to any international contest. However, the first four winners from the new Singh era made history by winning the right to represent the country in the Miss Universe pageant – an honour previously bestowed on the winners of the Morley-run Miss England, Scotland and Wales contests.

Thus Sarah Jane Southwick from Birmingham became the first ever Miss Great Britain to go on to the Miss Universe pageant in 1995, and one of only four titleholders to do so.

Singer Anita St Rose became the first black Miss Great Britain in 1996. She travelled to the USA for the Miss Universe pageant, but afterwards signed a recording contract which prevented her from carrying on as Miss Great Britain. Runner-up Liz Fuller, from Swansea, took over the title until 1998 and - as we will see - became personally involved with the Miss Great Britain brand for many years.

A chance encounter outside a London nightclub launched the career of the next winner. Leilani Dowding was a 19-year-old student when, while waiting for her boyfriend outside the Hippodrome, she was approached by an organiser of the Miss Great Britain pageant about to take place inside and invited to compete.

She did so, won the crown, and went on to the Miss Universe final in Hawaii. After her reign she enjoyed a career as a Page 3 girl, model and reality TV star, dated a string of soccer stars including Kieron Dyer, and finished 89th in *FHM*'s World's Sexiest poll.

Emma Spellar from Norwich took the crown in 2004 in London's Café de Paris and, with it, a host of prizes, including a holiday in Cuba and trip to China for the Model of the World final.

Yet nine months later she was telling the *Daily Star* of, "My Year of Hell as Miss GB."

Emma said she received neither of the trips she won, nor saw any sign of the £28,000 modelling contract that formed part of her prize, pointing out that she earned more money as a part-time beautician than as Miss Great Britain.

"It's been a nightmare," wailed Emma. "The airline that was meant to fly me out to Cuba for my holiday went bust, and I was told by the organisers that I didn't need a visa to fly to China for the Model of the World contest, even though I had been insisting for months that I did.

"I was told a week before departure that because I had no visa, I couldn't go. They promised me the world, but all I got were a few photoshoots and TV appearances – none of which were paid. All I've received in six months is a cheque for £1,000."

Emma said the situation was so bad that she had parted company with the Miss Great Britain organisers and returned to her beautician work in Norwich.

A Miss Great Britain spokesman refuted Emma's claims. "The reason she didn't go to China was because she decided to take a paying job at the last minute," he said. "And her trip to Cuba was postponed because the airline couldn't get permission to land at Gatwick. We sent her and her boyfriend to Spain instead. The PR team has done nothing wrong and it's very unfair to blame them."

The Miss Great Britain franchise was bought by businessman Robert de Keyser in 2006, in conjunction with Liz Fuller, who had won the title in 1997.

A fashion agent, de Keyser was responsible for hiring Victoria Beckham as a designer for his Rock & Republic brand of jeans. He and Liz relaunched the Miss Great Britain format by scrapping the age limit and introducing voting by both the live audience and by text message.

Misdemeanours Volume One – as well as many front page headlines – detailed the spectacular sacking of Danielle Lloyd as Miss Great Britain 2006. One of the judges that night was footballer Teddy Sheringham, and they quickly became an item. But an interview that Danielle gave to a magazine gave the impression that they had been a couple well before the actual Miss Great Britain pageant.

Not only that, but she posed nude for *Playboy* magazine, which broke the rules a second time.

After Robert de Keyser sacked Danielle, the shamed beauty queen appeared on *Celebrity Big Brother*, where she received further scorn from the public for the part she played in the bullying of actress Shilpa Shetty during their time in the house.

Readers of *The Sun* newspaper were invited to vote for their favourite from the original finalists to replace Danielle as Miss Great Britain, and they selected British-Indian model Pretti Desai, who had originally finished fifth in the contest.

In 2007, Danielle took Miss Great Britain Limited to court in a bid to clear her name of cheating, following a front page newspaper article – headlined "Miss Cheat Britain!" - being linked to the pageant website.

The organisation accepted that the incriminating interview that Danielle had given to *Eve* magazine was "untrue" and that she had not met Sheringham until after the pageant. As a result, Danielle dropped her libel claim.

In a further victory for Danielle, Liz Fuller – who took sole control from de Keyser of the Miss Great Britain organisation in 2009 – made the decision to reinstate the title to Danielle.

She told *The Sun*, "The contest is part of Danielle's history, and ours. There was no management or guidance afterwards and she ended up in *Playboy*. If there had been a management structure behind Miss Great Britain, she could have chosen a different route."

Danielle now shares the 2006 title on the pageant's website with Preeti Desai, who became a successful Bollywood actress.

Rachael Tennant is listed in the history books as having resigned as Miss Great Britain 2007.

The blonde from Aberdeen was working for an oil company when, on a whim, she entered the pageant online and found herself, not just in the final at London's Grosvenor Hotel, but announced as the winner, beating *Daily Star* Page 3 model Michelle Marsh, former Miss Wales Claire Evans and future *Desperate Scousewives* star Amanda Harrington.

Rachael's victory meant that she had to pull out of that year's Miss Scotland contest – the title that she had set her heart on. She had finished third in Miss Scotland the previous year and was hoping it would be second time lucky in 2007. Her win as Miss Great Britain put paid to her eligibility to take part and she admitted that she was "gutted".

"I never wanted to be Miss Great Britain," she told *The Sun*. "I mean it was fantastic and I'll never forget it, but I only ever wanted to be Miss Scotland."

When Miss Great Britain organiser Robert de Keyser admitted that he was having trouble finding a suitable venue for the 2008 pageant, he invited Rachael to stay on as the current titleholder until a new contest could be staged. Rachael, still hoping to pursue her Miss Scotland dream, refused his offer and stepped down, handing the crown to her runner-up Gemma Garrett.

"I've been honoured to have been Miss Great Britain for the past year," she said. "I am now thrilled to hand over my crown to my friend Gemma."

New winner Gemma quickly made a name for herself when stood as a candidate in the Crewe & Nantwich by-election on behalf of The Miss Great Britain Party, a new political party founded by de Keyser, with the aim of making Westminster "sexy, not sleazy".

The majority of the party's candidates were Miss Great Britain contestants, but it was titleholder Gemma who gained the most attention.

The Belfast model – who had previously won the Miss Ulster title in 1999 - finished tenth out of the ten Crewe & Nantwich candidates, but a creditable fifth out of the 26 standing for Haltemprice & Howden, with 521 votes.

She gave a lively interview to the *Daily Mail*, rejecting the idea of an alliance with Gordon Brown ("Have you ever seen that man smile?"), describing David Cameron as "hot, hot, hot", didn't recognise the name of any female politician except Margaret Thatcher, and called footballers "cocky, overconfident and contemptuous of women."

The Miss Great Britain Party's political life proved short, and was deregistered by the Electoral Commission a year later.

Gemma appeared on a BBC3 documentary – *Gemma Garrett: Are my Fake Breasts Safe?* - in 2012, in a bid to highlight to young women the dangers of cosmetic surgery, after doctors found that her PIP breast implants had ruptured, leaving silicone in her blood.

Gemma, who carved a name for herself as an actress, presenter and now newspaper and magazine columnist, married her long-term boyfriend in Belfast in 2010, but they separated four years later.

In 2009 Miss Great Britain boss Robert de Keyser married his fourth wife Hollie, 25, while his company, De Keyser Fashions, went into administration with debts of several million pounds, shortly after a well-publicised falling out with Victoria Beckham.

When Victoria terminated her relationship with Rock & Republic to launch her own fashion range, VB, she wanted to take the 'crown' logo with her, permission for which de Keyser refused, adding that her new range was "seriously overpriced."

As a result of de Keyser's financial situation, the 2009 pageant – due to be held in February in London – was postponed. The company behind the contest made a loss of £53,000 in 2006 and £62,000 in 2007.

Dave Reed, of PR company Neon Management held the 2009 final instead, organising a lavish show at the Café de Paris, London. They stimulated heavy media coverage, attracting 70,000 original entrants before whittling them down to a final 12.

The day before the final, the contestant touted as the hot favourite to win withdrew from the pageant, reportedly due to pressure from her boyfriend, R&B singer Craig David.

An insider told the *Daily Star* that finalist Francesca Neill had allegedly received a text message from David that led her to quit. "He wasn't happy about her taking part, and nor were her parents," the source added. "Francesca is devastated."

The couple split shortly afterwards and Francesca is now a top celebrity make-up artist, working on shows such as *The X Factor, Strictly Come Dancing* and *Britain's Got Talent.*

The 2009 final was won by Newcastle marketing director Sophie Gradon, with judges including footballer Paul Gascoigne and singer Simon Webbe.

Shortly after the crowning, Liz Fuller bought the Miss Great Britain franchise from Robert de Keyser and inherited Sophie as her first winner. It proved not to be the easiest of starts when a row erupted on social media concerning a penalty train fare the beauty queen had incurred while attending a photo shoot for a skincare brand.

The skincare company had liaised directly with Sophie as to which train times suited her, and had booked and paid for the tickets. However, when Sophie decided to board an earlier more expensive train, she was fined £70 by the ticket inspector. She passed the fine on to the Miss Great Britain head office and was incensed when they refused to pay it.

A statement on the Miss Great Britain website read, "Sophie Gradon will not be attending the final on Saturday. She has been demanding that Miss GB pay a train fare she incurred because she boarded the wrong train. Miss GB cannot encourage irresponsible behaviour and will not be paying any train fines, parking fines, library fines, etc."

Sophie hit back on Facebook, saying, "In my experience, Miss GB is full of false hope and false promises. It shouldn't be speculated that girls will be given such opportunities until they actually happen."

She later told the *Daily Star Sunday*, "I'm absolutely disgusted to find out it wouldn't be paid. I got a court summons from the rail company and now I'm being asked to pay £150. I did so much work as Miss Great Britain and I thought they would pay my train ticket."

New owner Liz Fuller told the newspaper that, "Sophie will not be welcome at the 2010 ceremony as she has created a lot of bad feelings and has behaved in a very irresponsible way. As far as we know, she just couldn't be bothered to get on the right train."

As for allegations from Sophie that no opportunities had been created for her, Liz was happy to put the record straight. "That was unfair of Sophie. We got her photo shoots, personal appearances and a three-page spread in *OK!* Magazine. We would've got her more if she hadn't tried to abuse her position, asking the ticket inspector, 'Don't you know who I am?' and saying that Miss Great Britain should travel for free."

Sophie even went so far as to sue the organisation in court over the £70 fine. She lost her case.

"What is it with these girls that they believe nothing is their fault?" Liz Fuller asked.

Speaking to the author recently, Sophie admitted that she had been "young and naïve" during her reign, and that she "probably did get on the wrong train – I'm hopeless at organising myself!"

Of her year as Miss Great Britain, she said, "Dave Reed at Neon Management was a great guy, but had a different vision of how he saw the winner. He wanted to go more down the glamour route.

"I did a shoot with *Nuts* magazine with some beautiful lingerie, and had agreed not to go topless. In the shoot I was coerced into doing 'implied topless' - my boobs were covered, often with my hands. Needless to say all the pics in the mag were of me with my bra off and the shots of me with my bra on were simply the 'warm up'.

"I made the mistake of reading the readers' comments online – 'skinny fat', 'ugly', 'looks like a man in drag' – and it made me near suicidal, it made me hate myself."

Sophie says that Liz Fuller taking over the franchise was 'like a breath of fresh air', yet she found that "being treated like a piece of meat at functions, someone to be looked at and touched, and for remarks to made about my looks, made me realise that I didn't have the thick skin necessary to be a beauty queen or model.

"I decided then that I no longer wanted to be judged simply on how I looked, and I returned to my studies and a more normal life. After all, I have a brain, I have feelings – people seem to forget that!"

In 2016, Sophie joined the cast of ITV2's *Love Island*, a reality show in which single men and women were flown out to a luxury villa in

Mallorca, where cameras would capture every second of budding romances and furious rows.

Sophie paired up with Welsh barman Tom Powell and were seen enjoying an intimate moment inside a wardrobe, leaving little to the viewers' imagination despite their attempts to avoid the cameras. Despite their tempestuous relationship on the show, they stayed together as a couple after leaving the villa, before finally splitting later that year.

When Liz Fuller purchased the Miss Great Britain franchise midway through 2009, she lifted the ban on divorcees and unmarried mothers in a bid to make the competition "more relevant to today's society."

"Pageants have too long been a male-dominated business with little regard for the real interest of the girls who enter", she said.

The first divorcee to take part in the history of the contest was Rachel Hatton, a single parent who qualified for the Miss Great Britain 2010 final after winning the Miss Warwickshire pageant.

She didn't win but Rachel, a former telecommunications specialist in the British Army, only had to wait two more years before her next foray into the newspapers. In 2012, she stood trial in Northampton Crown Court, accused of falsely claiming £22,000 worth of benefits as a single parent when, it was alleged, she was living with her boyfriend.

The prosecution alleged that Rachel, with her small son, was living with boyfriend Nathaniel Simon at his four-bedroom house in Northampton, while telling the Benefits Office that he was merely her landlord.

Rachel told the court that they had never been in a relationship, despite sleeping together "a couple of times", yet wasn't charged by Simon for any utility bills, had been insured to drive his car, and that they had been on holiday together to Turkey.

At the end of the week-long trial both she and Simon were found not guilty of benefits fraud, and she wept in the dock with relief.

Liz Fuller may well look back at the 2010 pageant as a whole and come to the conclusion that it was cursed, following a succession of negative newspaper articles concerning some of her contestants.

The adverse media coverage began with the sacking of the winner of the Central London heat. Lora Jayne Nuttall was stripped of her sash hours after winning when organisers found photos on her Facebook page socialising with former *Big Brother* contestant, Rex Newmark, who had been one of the judges that night.

Although their year-long relationship had ended several months beforehand, Liz Fuller was furious. She said, "I was left with no choice but to strip Lora of her Miss Central London title because of what Rex did – he was completely unprofessional.

"The judges assured me they were impartial, but on the night there was no impartiality from him."

It also emerged that Lora knew one of the other judges, TV fashion presenter Julian Bennett. "Julian not only knew Lora, but he also behaved very rudely," said Liz. "He was even shouting obscenities at some of the girls while they were being interviewed."

Lora said she was "devastated" at losing her title. "I didn't know Rex was on the panel until the contest was about to start, and when I saw him my heart sank. Having an ex on the panel is the last thing you want. I've had some horrible emails from girls who think I was trying to win unfairly, but I wasn't."

Liz Fuller declared that she was considering all-female judging panels in future, and that the Central London heat would be run again, admitting to *The Sun*, "It was a bad start for someone who had promised to reintroduce ethics to the pageant."

Next, came the story of 27-year-old Laura Anness, who arguably goes down in history as the only beauty queen to be stripped of two titles within as many months. Laura originally made the press that summer when she was disqualified from the Miss England pageant for lying about her age.

Having told the organisers she was only 22, she won the Miss Cornwall title and her true age was only exposed when the Miss England organiser found entry forms from three previous years, all stating the same age. The Miss England rules stated at that time that contestants must be aged between 17 and 24. Laura also admitted to being a single mother, another contravention of the Miss England rules, and furthermore that she lived in Devon, not Cornwall as required.

She was summarily sacked as Miss Cornwall.

However, taking advantage of Miss Great Britain's permitted age range of 18 to 29, and the fact that it was open to single mothers, she took part in, and won, the Plymouth heat, giving her entry into the final in Weston-super-Mare that November.

Organiser Liz told the press, "I think Laura has had a really difficult time. She made that one mistake with her age. She just wants that break and this is her second chance."

The press loved this story of redemption – but that warm glow of a happy ending wasn't to last. Two months later, the *Daily Express* reported that Laura Anness had been exposed as a former prostitute. The article alleged that she had posed topless for a Sunday newspaper in 1999 and revealed how she had worked in a massage parlour at the age of 16, earning up to £400 a week.

"They told me I'd have to do extras," she told the reporter at the time. "I thought I'd give it a try."

Liz Fuller, upon hearing of the dubious past of one of her finalists – and, furthermore, one whom she had only just 'saved' - stripped her of her Miss Plymouth title immediately.

"I'm shocked," Liz told the *Express*. "Miss GB must be a good role model for female society."

But the drama was far from over. Shirlena Johnson had already competed in three heats of the 2010 pageant and each time had given her age as 28.

However, the singer's true age was uncovered when Shirlena's audition for ITV's *The X Factor* talent show was shown that summer. Performing a bizarre version of Duffy's hit single *Mercy*, Shirlena was shown clawing at the floor and growling at the camera.

"You're completely crazy, but I like that," said head judge Simon Cowell after her audition. "You're fantastically nuts."

But just days later *X Factor* executives, on the advice of the programme's medical experts, took the decision not to allow her to continue in the audition process, over concerns for her mental health.

The show had given her age as thirty, a year over the Miss Great Britain upper limit. Once more, Liz Fuller was forced to step in and ban her from the pageant, while at pains to explain that the decision was purely down to age.

"Shirlena turned up in a ballerina outfit one time, and a sari another time," she told the press. "We have a vigorous interview policy to assess our girls, and we didn't doubt Shirlena's mental ability at all. She came to three heats and even though she never made the top five, we found her to be strong, ambitious and astute. It's a shame to lose her."

The stress of facing one drama after another made Liz ill with suspected pneumonia just before the final but, as she told *The Sun*, "I ignored it, I couldn't be ill."

Former Miss World Rosanna Davison was among the judges for the lavish black tie grand final in Weston-super-Mare, yet even the show itself was beset with problems.

Liz told *The Sun*, "Just as I was announcing the final 12, a producer ran to the side of the stage and told me he had forgotten to include the winner of the public phone and text vote. So, rather embarrassingly, we had to have a top 13 and, even though we had made her a finalist instead, I realised I would have to refund her family the £2,000 they had spent on voting for her."

Even with the beleaguered contest safely over, poor Liz was to face yet more acrimony.

Hours after Liverpool law student Amy Carrier took the crown, irate fans and losing contestants and their families vented their disgust online, accusing Liz Fuller of fixing the result.

An article in the *Daily Star Sunday* reported that one claimed: "Yes, Liz Fuller, your competition is a BIG FIX. Liz Fuller picked the top 25, not the judges. Liz Fuller picked the winner."

Another raged, "Absolute joke, this competition! I was there and I heard the organisers say that the judges' opinions were not needed and that the organisers would pick the winner."

Liz refuted these claims in the strongest possible terms. "The top 25 were chosen by the judges in a pre-interview judging session that lasted over five hours," she said. "Each of the five judges met each contestant for 5-10 minutes, asking them important questions and allowing their Facebook pages to be studied in order to assess their character.

"The interview process went on until 1am because it was so important for us to find a great ambassador and a genuinely nice girl. We didn't want another beautiful girl with an ugly personality."

She reiterated these views in the *Daily Star*. "I've had loads of abuse since the results. But the comments are coming from sore losers and bitches. Some of them may be confused as to why certain girls didn't make the final 12. We weren't looking for just beauty, but girls who had character too. I wanted a girl who the others could look up to. Amy was the perfect winner."

"I saw some sights on some of their Facebook pages," she said. "There were pictures of some getting drunk, status updates with swearing, details of the men they've slept with. That is not the sort of girl we were looking for."

Liz revealed later that some of the finalists were so upset that they had threatened to write her name on escort cards and place them in phone booths.

She had been dealt a blow three months earlier, when a deal she was about to strike with Channel 5 to screen the pageant fell through, after TV executives decided to take the *Big Brother* programme instead after it was dropped by Channel 4.

Despite the Weston-super-Mare final being profitable, and featured on many TV shows and in the press, at the beginning of 2011, Liz Fuller decided enough was enough and she sold the company.

Under the headline, "Miss GBH", Liz gave her story to *The Sun* as to how her dream of reviving the pageant turned into fourteen months of hell.

In the piece she wrote herself, she said, "I did meet some beautiful and talented girls, but I also met a never-ending parade of girls whose ultimate aspiration is instant fame or WAGdom. Most had two things in common: Jordan was their heroine, and they were bad losers."

Describing the girls who had posed topless, enjoyed relationships with the judges, lied about their ages, and spats with family members unhappy at the results, she said, "It sounds like 'Carry On Up The Catwalk', but the consequences have been serious. It dented my belief in others and my sense of fair play.

"One PR company even asked me to fix the result so that a girlfriend of a sportsman on their books would win. Those fourteen months cost me my health and any chance of a personal life or serious relationship. It also cost me my peace of mind.

"I now know how the beauty industry works — inside and out — and it's not an experience I want to repeat."

Liz told the author, "I was a judge or presenter at every Miss Great Britain pageant from 1999 to 2006, so I saw and heard just as many issues as I went through; what shocked me was finding out who was causing these issues. To be told that one of the sweetest of girls had a background in prostitution was such a shock. It proves how important background checks on the contestants are.

"It's also easy for a contestant to put on an act or put forward a certain persona for the judges. An organisation or judge has to be able to evaluate and analyse this."

Liz handed the Miss Great Britain licence back to the Singh brothers and left to go and live in the States, where she forged a successful career as an actress and TV presenter. She is also the CEO of Miss British Empire, a pageant she launched in 2011.

American former model and professional matchmaker Wendy Seinturier had been working alongside Liz Fuller as the pageant's Etiquette and Runway coach, and bought the licence from the Singhs. However, when she sacked Miss York City, Charlotte Campbell, for posing for 'implied nude' photos, she faced a storm of undesired press attention.

Wendy alleged to have possession of fully-nude photos of single mother Charlotte, an allegation the beauty queen denied vehemently. Wendy said she felt unsupported by the pageant owners and stepped down as CEO, whereupon Charlotte's title was restored to her.

Yet again, the Miss Great Britain ship was suddenly left without an anchor, and there was no pageant held in either 2011 or 2012.

Salvation came in the form of another former beauty queen. Kate Solomons-Freakley had been both a Miss England runner-up and host when, in 2005, she founded ModelZed, a modelling and events agency based in her home town of Leicester, and since rebranded as The Kreative Group.

Kate had dreamed of running a major beauty pageant and her chance came in 2012 when she and colleague Jemma Simmonds took on the franchise for Miss Great Britain from John Singh, with the winner representing the country in the final of the Miss Tourism World pageant.

Their tenure heralded yet another new chapter in the turbulent Miss Great Britain story, and Kate's intention was to run a pageant free from the sleaze, controversy and allegations that had sullied its reputation over the past twenty years. It was a vow that was, through no fault of her own, going to prove difficult to keep.

There had never been a kiss and tell story in the pageant's history, so it was therefore bad luck on Kate's part when the winner from 2001 decided to come along as a guest to the 2014 event.

As in 2013, the pageant was being held at the Athena, a former art deco cinema and now conferencing and banqueting venue in Leicester. One of the judges was millionaire businessman Duncan Bannatyne, the 66-year-old star of the BBC's hugely successful *Dragons' Den*. During the evening he got chatting to beautiful blonde Michelle Evans, Miss Great Britain 2001, who was there as a guest of licence owner John Singh.

Both Duncan and Michelle were recently divorced and, soon after that evening, were pictured in the press having nights out in each other's company. Both looked happy and content, and ModelZed must've wondered if they had their first wedding on their hands.

That is, until three months later, when the press showed photos of Duncan coming out of a London restaurant with a woman who most definitely wasn't Michelle. The lady on his arm was a stunning 36-year-old from Uzbekistan called Nigora Whitehorn whom, he later revealed, he had met at the reception of a Harley Street dental practice.

The first Michelle knew of Duncan's transference of affections was the publication of these pictures, and she was not pleased. Just 24 hours earlier she had tweeted a thanks to him for her birthday champagne and roses, but now she returned to her Twitter account to parody her former boyfriend's *Dragons' Den* sign-off, with a defiant, "I'm out!"

Infuriated by Duncan's casual attitude – he tweeted, "Love is in the air!" next to a photo of him with his new girlfriend - Michelle sought to redress the balance after such public humiliation. Texting him to ask for a contribution towards the £1,200 in childcare she had paid out while they were dating, he replied telling her "not to cause trouble" on her social media site, and when she protested that she was just speaking the truth, he went on to ask if she would "be happy with me showing the pictures you sent me?"

'Violated' at the thought of the three lingerie-clad and naked pictures she had sent Duncan early in their relationship being shared, Michelle went to the press.

The front page of the *Mail on Sunday* told of: "The revenge porn dragon: Duncan Bannatyne made me send him naked photos, then threatened to show them to the world, says beauty queen who dumped him."

"I thought the betrayal and public humiliation of being cheated on was as bad as it would get", she told the newspaper, "but then he threatened me with something so personal, I was in complete shock.

"He made me feel like I was the one who had done something wrong for sending him personal pictures that HE asked for. He made me think he was going to share them with the world. I sent them believing we'd be together forever, but as soon as things didn't go his way things turned sour. I feel disgusted and disappointed."

The story went on to say how he had asked her within ten minutes of their first date if she wanted more children, that he was such dull company he often invited employees out with them for meals, and that for Christmas he gave her a £20 gift box from his own Bannatyne Spa wrapped in a Morrisons carrier bag.

"I feel like I was gullible," Michelle told the *Mail*, "but I guess I had a lucky escape. He will use every bit of mileage out of his fame to treat women like this."

From his romantic break in Paris, Duncan tweeted, "I hear there is a bunny boiler on the loose in the UK. I have no respect for anyone who sells a kiss and tell story for £25,000 and fills it with lies."

Upon his return he dragged Nigora onto the set of ITV's *This Morning* a few days later to declare that he didn't feel bitter about the revelations because he was "madly in love", while his girlfriend swooned that "he is the most generous man I have ever met in my life...I'm very much in love."

In November 2015, Duncan entered the jungle as a contestant for ITV's *I'm A Celebrity...Get Me Out of Here*, donating his six-figure fee to the Operation Smile charity in Africa. He and Nigora became engaged the following spring, marrying in a romantic beach ceremony in Portugal in June 2017.

Shelby Tribble faced the worst kind of insult after she had been crowned Miss Great Britain 2014. Czech website *Extra.cz* claimed that Shelby was not beautiful enough to have won the title, printing her photo with her face pixelated out.

"Great Britain has a new Miss and she proves the rule that British women are not beautiful," the website declared.

It was a cruel blow for the stunning 21-year-old from Plymouth, who had already revealed that she had been painfully shy at school and subjected to constant bullying. Shelby gained huge support from her online fans after the attack, and had the last laugh by winning a coveted spot in the Monster Energy Girls squad, appearing at stock car race tracks all over the country. She also went on to finish as fourth runner-up at the Miss Tourism World final in Malaysia.

The Miss Great Britain pageant celebrated its 70th anniversary in September 2015, inviting former title-holders and judges to commemorate the country's longest running beauty contest. Perhaps wisely, both Duncan Bannatyne and Michelle Evans declined their invitations.

However, as we saw in Chapter 1, the celebrations would soon be tarnished by one of the biggest controversies the pageant had faced in the whole of its seven decades.

The Miss Great Britain story – with its twists, turns and front-page headlines - was far from over.

Julia Lemigova, Miss USSR 1990

"My loss is with me every day, every single moment of the day"

When tennis legend Martina Navratilova married Julia Lemigova in a lavish ceremony just before Christmas 2014, one would've expected tabloid headlines referring to a "love match" at the very least.

Yet what we got instead was more celebrity juice than celebrity deuce.

"Meet Mrs Navratilova: the beauty queen with the VERY ugly past", was one such headline, as reporters pounced with glee on a back story that took in murder, prostitution and the tragic and mysterious death of a baby.

Martina's own past has been documented many times over the years. The nine times Wimbledon Singles Champion is a tennis legend, regularly named as the greatest female player in history with a total haul of 59 Grand Slam wins.

Born in 1956 in what was then Czechoslovakia, she won her first Wimbledon Singles championship in 1978 and became an American citizen three years later. Yet Martina's tumultuous love life proved almost as fascinating to the public as her record-breaking career on court.

She first identified herself as bisexual (and in later years as a lesbian) in a newspaper interview shortly after receiving her Green Card in 1981, an admission almost unheard of in the sports world in those days, and one which caused a huge backlash among the public and in the media. It also cost her millions of dollars in sponsorship and endorsement due to the corporate homophobia of the era.

Even today, in far more enlightened times, Martina laments that so few athletes have identified themselves as gay. "I can't believe that there has never been a male tennis player who has taken that step," she said.

In 1984, Martina began a seven-year relationship with Judy Nelson, a former Miss Texas, which ended in a much-publicised legal wrangle when Judy sued Martina in a multi-million dollar palimony suit, which was finally settled out of court.

Martina faced yet another lawsuit from ex-lover Toni Layton when their eight-year relationship ended abruptly in 2008. Toni filed a 'domestic partnership' suit on the opening day of Wimbledon 2009 for the "emotional, physical and mental trauma" caused by the sudden split.

A year later, the lawsuit was settled out of court for an alleged figure of £2.1m. This sum was largely seen as hush money in order to quell Toni's threat to tell all. "There are a lot of skeletons in Martina's closet," she had said at the time of lawsuit. "It is more like a storage facility full of them, and I know them all."

With such a chequered love life behind her, it was no surprise that Martina chose to keep her next girlfriend's name out of the press for as long as she could.

It was only during her appearance as a contestant on ITV's *I'm a Celebrity...Get Me Out of Here* game show in the autumn of 2008 that Martina spoke of her 'drop dead beautiful' girlfriend, leading to much speculation as to her identity.

All was finally revealed the following August, when Martina was photographed on holiday in the south of France with a statuesque and stunning lady identified as 36 year old Yuliya 'Julia' Lemigova. This was the first time that the couple had been photographed in public, and the media went wild with the speculation that they had already become engaged, a rumour which turned out to be false.

But more reasons soon emerged for the fascination the press had with Martina's new love. Not only was Julia a former beauty queen, but she came with a very complicated, very murky past.

Back in the USSR, President Gorbachev's *Perestroika* – the political movement bringing far-reaching changes and reform to the Soviet Union – resulted, in 1989, in a Miss USSR pageant being held for the first time in the vast nation's history.

The winner, Yuliya Sukhanova, made headlines for her historic first, but due to her tender age of 17 her parents refused permission to allow her to compete in the Miss World contest. However, shortly after coming of age she moved to the States, where she was seen partying with Donald Trump and guests aboard his £60m luxury yacht.

It was left to Yuliya's runner-up, Anna Gorbunova, to become the USSR's first representative at the Miss World pageant, where she was chosen as Miss Photogenic by photographers covering the event. Meanwhile, the USSR made its debut at Miss Universe in 1990, when another of the 1989 finalists, Evija Stalbovska, made the final 15 of the pageant held in Los Angeles.

Julia Lemigova, the daughter of a colonel in the aviation field – and not, as some newspapers reported, a high-ranking general in the KGB - didn't actually win the Miss USSR title in 1990. The last pageant before the collapse of the Soviet Union saw the crown go to Mariya Kezha from Belarus, who turned her back on the title by deciding she wanted to get married instead. The crown therefore went to runner-up Julia, who became the last ever Miss USSR.

A final pageant, Miss Soviet Union, took place amidst the chaos of the fall of the USSR in 1991, after which many of the separate states held pageants as independent countries in their own right.

But before that, Julia travelled to Las Vegas for the 1991 Miss Universe contest, where she became a press favourite and was compared in looks to actress Julia Roberts. She finished as second runner-up, giving the USSR its best placing in its short beauty pageant existence.

In the final question round involving the last three remaining candidates, she was asked what the biggest problem facing her country at that time was. Julia replied, "I think, I hope, all the problems in my country are over now. Everything is free, and people are happy – and I'm happy!"

However happy she may have seemed at the pageant, she was keen to seek a better life for herself and, using her title as a platform, she left post-Soviet Russia to base herself in London. The press was fascinated by the lady they dubbed 'the final export from the defunct Soviet Union', and she was easily able to charm herself into the right social circles.

Arriving in London, she told the *Daily Express*, "I don't really have the Miss USSR title anymore because there is no more Soviet Union. But it is thanks to Mr Gorbachev that I was able to take part in a beauty contest in the first place. His *Perestroika* changed so much. It changed my life.

"I worked hard in the big fashion houses in Moscow and travelled to Italy and Japan to push Russian fabrics. Now my ambition is to reach the top in the States and to travel back home modelling London designs in the snow in Red Square. Every week I try to speak to my parents who keep me in touch with the latest news from my country. It is the only time I get to hear Russian."

Naim Attallah, then Chief Executive of The Asprey Group, remembers first meeting Julia in London in 1991, when she arrived at a party on the arm of actress Joanna Lumley's ex-husband, Jeremy Lloyd. Naim invited Julia to model a 24-carat wedding dress, valued at £180,000, as part of Asprey's *Celebration of Gold* exhibition. According to the press, she "caused a sensation and sent the photographers into a frenzy with her beguiling Caucasian beauty."

Taking financial advice from her new friend Sir James Goldsmith, Julia moved to Paris in the mid-nineties, where she set up a cosmetics and beauty company named *Russie Blanche* (White Russia) and opened a luxury spa. In 1997, she met banker Edouard Stern, a married father of three named as the 38th wealthiest man in France and a close associate of the then President Nicholas Sarkozy. They met in secret in hotels all over the world until Stern left his wife a year later.

In 1999, Julia gave birth to their son, Maximilien, but Stern showed little interest in his son and at one point questioned whether he was the boy's true father. There, Julia's story took a desperately dark and tragic turn. In March 2000, Maximilien died aged just five months, his cause of death alleged to have been due to brain injuries but never proven.

The tragedy happened just days after Stern had employed a Bulgarian nanny to look after their son, and when he was in his father's care at the time. The nanny – known only as Maya - vanished immediately after the baby's death and has never been found.

A distraught Julia demanded to know if Stern had paid the nanny to murder their son but the inquiry into his death was closed in 2002 due to lack of evidence.

Just three years later, Edouard Stern was found shot dead in his apartment in Geneva, having been murdered by a prostitute called Cecile Brossard, Stern's long-term mistress, during a sadomasochistic bondage session.

When Stern was found dead dressed head-to-toe in a latex catsuit and tied to a chair in his apartment, 40-year-old Brossard confessed to the murder "in a moment of madness" after Stern had allegedly tormented her over a million dollar gift he was threatening to take back. The courtroom heard that Stern had told her that, "A million dollars is a lot to pay for a whore."

Brossard was sentenced to eight and a half years in prison for the murder, of which she served five.

There had long been rumours that Stern took part in sexual orgies alongside some of France's most powerful figures, fuelling claims of a high-level cover-up that has prevented the truth being exposed of not only his death — but that of his and Julia's son, Maximilien.

Fresh evidence came to light in 2010, when a previously suppressed autopsy report showed traces of the anti-depressant diazepam in the baby's blood. It was also revealed that the nanny had written a note in which she expressed fears for the little boy's life.

Both Julia and the police believe Cecile Brossard holds the key to the truth, but she remains "frightened and uncooperative", according to a legal source, vowing to remain silent about her life with Stern, a move that gives further credence to theories of a cover-up.

Julia gave birth to two daughters in later years from two separate relationships - yet she remains "extremely frustrated and disappointed" that she has been denied justice for Maximilien. Her lawyer said, "All she wants is the truth – she needs to know what happened to her son."

After so much turbulence and anguish for Julia, it must have come as a supreme comfort to meet and settle down with a figure as respected and lauded as Martina Navratilova. Martina had made no secret of the fact that she dreamed of getting married – "to the right person" – especially after her own battle with breast cancer in 2010.

They had first met at a dinner party during the French Open in Paris in 2001 while Julia was pursuing a modelling career. They had chatted and got on well, but it would be eight more years before they would meet again, once more in Paris. Their friendship, Julia told the *Daily Mail*, was platonic at first and Martina would come round and play tennis with Julia's daughters Victoria and Emma. "The girls adored her," she said, "Marti, as they call her, was just part of the family right from the off."

The girls never questioned their mother's relationship with Martina, but when the older girl came home from school one day, upset at things that had been said by her classmates, they sat both daughters down to explain that they were in love. There have since been discussions about Martina adopting the girls one day to complete the family.

So the proposal of marriage, when it came, was always going to be very special. Martina was commentating at the US Open tennis championships in September 2014 and, during a break in the men's semi-final, she beckoned Julia over, went down on bended knee, and brandished a ring.

"We've been together for over six years," Martina said, "and I can't imagine my life without you. So Julia Lemigova, will you please do me the honour...will you please marry me?" The moment was flashed live on the big screens on court and the crowd roared with approval.

As she waited for Julia to accept, Martina joked, "Is that a yes? My knee's killing me!"

Despite the family living in Florida, state laws at that time banned same-sex marriage, so the couple married in New York in December 2014 with Julia's daughters in attendance. "I had to look at the ceiling to stop myself from crying," Julia said of the emotional ceremony.

The family still split their time between the States and France, where Julia continues to run her company. "The girls speak French to each other," said Julia, "English to Martina, and Russian to me!"

Julia refused to elaborate on the mystery surrounding the death of Maximilien, but said she will never forget him. "My loss is with me every day, every single moment of the day," she told the *Daily Mail*. "I shared that with Martina – it was part of me, my pain, my grief."

In July 2015, Julia was invited by ITV chat show host Lorraine Kelly to join her on the sofa where she talked with great charm about life as a woman married to one of the tennis world's greatest names, and the fact that the US Supreme Court had, a month earlier, made same-sex marriage a legal right across the whole of America.

"It's an amazing feeling to know that a family like ours can be legal now, and there is no more of that nonsense that love between two women is any less meaningful than a love between a man and a woman," she told Lorraine.

A few months later the couple appeared on quiz show *All-Star Mr & Mrs* where their obvious devotion to each other shone through. "We feel safe with each other," said Martina. "It just works."

Julia is amused but delighted to be seen as the David Furnish of the lesbian world, a poster girl for same-sex marriage. Mindful of the fact that gay marriage is still an inflammatory issue in her native Russia and in many other parts of the world, Julia knows there are many barriers to overcome.

"But I think seeing couples like us marry is important," she said. "I really hope it gives encouragement to families like ours."

Miss South Africa 1991-2015

"Any victory for one black South African is a victory for us all"
President Nelson Mandela

The Miss World organisation took the decision in 1977 to ban South Africa from competing as result of its continuing policy of apartheid.

Only once the constraints of such a political system were seen to have visibly loosened enough to satisfy the international community was the country tentatively welcomed back onto the world stage – including South Africa's return to the Miss World pageant.

But that first, newly-launched Miss South Africa pageant could hardly claim to be a symbol of the new fairness and equality being trumpeted by the government to the rest of the world. In a country with five times as many black people as white, only fifty of the five hundred contestants were black – with only one, a multi-racial woman, reaching the final twelve.

The panel of nine judges – eight of whom were white – chose Diana Tilden-Davis, a tall, blonde actress, as the first Miss South Africa to represent her country at the Miss World finals for fourteen years.

Diana's half-sister Janine had won the Miss South Africa crown in 1988, and a second half-sister Leanne had made the finals in 1982. Yet despite murmurs of disapproval from the black community over her victory, it was Diana herself who ignited controversy when she joined her fellow Miss World contestants in the USA.

Miss Nigeria, Abenike Oshinowo, reportedly asked her why more black women didn't compete in Miss South Africa. According to Miss

Nigeria, Diana replied that the reason was because "most black girls become pregnant by the time they're 15."

"It was an ugly and insensitive thing to say," said Abenike.

When the story hit the press, Diana denied she had made the remark. Miss World chairman Julia Morley dismissed the report as "a vicious and mischievous rumour" and that Diana's remarks had been "taken out of context".

Despite the unwelcome publicity, Diana finished third in the Miss World pageant in Atlanta, Georgia.

She once again made worldwide news in 2003 when she was mauled in the leg by a hippopotamus while canoeing in Botswana, where she was living with her husband and daughter. Diana underwent six operations and was considered lucky to have escaped with her life. She was still walking with the aid of crutches two years after the attack.

In 1992, the Morleys made a controversial decision to move the Miss World pageant to a region of the world which they themselves had refused to recognise as an independent state and from which they had banned any representative from taking part.

Bophuthatswana was, however – as a state independent from South Africa - a magnet for the sort of gambling and adult entertainment banned under South African rule.

And so it was that hotel magnate Sol Kerzner, CEO of Sun International and ex-husband of Miss World 1974 Anneline Kriel, chose the area in which to open his vast Sun City resort and casino.

The resort was opened in 1979 yet many of the biggest music stars of the day refused to play at Sun City, considering it representative of all apartheid's evils, surrounded as it was by the poverty and deprivation of the black homelands.

Indeed, in 1985 artists such as Bruce Springsteen, Bob Dylan, Ringo Starr, Lou Reed, Peter Gabriel, Pete Townsend and U2, among others, formed a one-off collaborative called Artists United Against Apartheid and released the single *(I Ain't Gonna Play) Sun City*, raising over $1m for anti-apartheid projects.

Sun City's new Palace of the Lost City resort – which cost an estimated $350m to build - was the opulent setting for the Miss World final on five occasions – from 1992-1995, and again in 2001.

In her book, *Broadcasting the End of Apartheid: Live Television and the Birth of the New South Africa*, Martha Evans wrote of the Morleys' "extraordinary decision" to sign a three-year deal with Sol Kerzner. Kerzner was, she said, paid a one-off sum to host and produce the show, receiving television rights in return, and securing three years of global marketing for Sun City.

Martha Evans wrote that the combination of the lavish Sun City setting and Kerzner's talent for staging spectacles would, the Morleys hoped, give a boost to Miss World's sliding popularity and ensure its return to terrestrial TV for the first time since 1988, especially as the 1991 pageant in Atlanta had lost them money.

Journalist Zoe Heller commented at the time that the contract was mutually beneficial, based on the shared 'empathy of pariahs'.

History was made that same year when Amy Kleinhans became the first non-white Miss South Africa in its 40-year history.

Amy, of mixed race heritage, had competed in 1991 and finished as first runner-up, before going one step further a year later and taking the crown. Her win had been predicted before the pageant, due to criticism that a non-white woman had never won, but she shrugged off the rumours.

"The controversy surrounding me because of my skin colour means nothing," she said.

Amy's prize was to represent her country in the Miss World pageant in Sun City. During the preliminary parade of nations, she refused to walk with the flag of the-then apartheid South Africa, and instead chose a white flag as a symbol of peace. After the pageant – in which she finished fifth – she received a call from Nelson Mandela to thank her for her thoughtfulness and bravery.

But it wasn't quite the fairytale portrayed on television and in the press, and TV producer Mark West laid bare the bitter truth in an interview with the South African *Sunday Times*.

"The day after she won Miss South Africa at Sun City, she and her mother drove back to Cape Town," he recalled. "They had to sleep in the car. They weren't allowed into any hotels or motels because she was a coloured girl."

In 1996, Amy was arrested and charged with shoplifting a cheap lipstick from a pharmacy, charges she denied and which were eventually dropped.

A qualified teacher and successful businesswoman, Amy established the Dial-a-Teacher service in 1998, giving schoolchildren access to a bank of retired teachers to help and advise on homework, studies and exams. Its patron was Nelson Mandela until his death in 2013.

Interest in the Miss South Africa pageant itself had fallen since the end of apartheid. As one social commentator explained, "The competition used to be all about celebrating blonde Aryan beauties. Black South Africans have far less interest in pageants than white South Africans, so interest took a dip."

But enthusiasm was to be revived on a mass scale when, in 1993, Jacqui Palesa Mofokeng, from Soweto, was crowned the first black winner of the Miss South Africa pageant, thus completing the transformation of a nation.

"If you watch the show back," she said of hearing her name announced, "you actually see me staggering. I saw stars and was blinded at that moment. That was a God moment for me. I didn't know it then, but I do now."

Jacqui's father, an executive for EMI Records, sent his daughter to a private multi-racial school in a white area, but despite a relatively privileged upbringing, she never forgot her responsibility to the black community. "I know tonight, as I sit here with a crown on my head, that there are people dying in the townships. I have not forgotten them," she said after her victory.

Nelson Mandela was one of the first to congratulate Jacqui. "Any victory for one black South African is a victory for us all," he proclaimed.

Yet while black South Africa celebrated such a momentous occasion in their history, *Rapport* – a Sunday newspaper and co-sponsor of the pageant – was inundated with calls within minutes of her crowning to protest the judges' decision, while their Letters page was filled with those accusing the pageant of being "rigged" and "blackwashed".

A local Johannesburg newspaper published a cartoon of Jacqui in her Miss South Africa crown with the caption, "Don't get carried away – you still can't vote". (In fact, the first election allowing all races to vote took place just months later, in April 1994).

Callers to a Johannesburg radio show said quite openly that Jacqui had a "big bum" and "ugly teeth", while her local Soweto press denounced the critics for making her life "absolute hell".

Jacqui told the *news24* website that she wasn't at all surprised by the race controversy that followed her crowning. "I disturbed – destroyed – the status quo of how beauty was defined by the previous establishment," she said. "There were times when it hurt, badly, but that did not stop me from being who I am."

She recalled a visit to the Chamber of Commerce early in her reign, where her reception was initially "very cold – as though they were trying to make sense of me. I felt like a fish in a bowl. However, by the time I left, all faces were smiles and most of the people in that room gave me hugs. I guess that is one of the reasons I became Miss South Africa, to have the racial stigma broken so that we can all see each other as people who live in South Africa together, not as enemies."

Jacqui didn't feel the need to keep her strong opinions to herself: She was in favour of abortion rights, against the tradition of paying for brides, and even let it be known that she supported the right of black democracy campaigners to disrupt the Miss World pageant in Sun City, in which she would compete.

"It's very legitimate," she said, "It's the one thing that will make people listen."

Jacqui finished as first runner-up in Miss World, and Nelson Mandela invited her onto the board of the Nelson Mandela Children's Fund. "There were times when he would call me on my cellphone," Jacqui laughs, "but I never got used to it. Every time he called, the whole world would stop."

In 2003, Jacqui moved to the States and now lives quietly in New Jersey with her American husband and two children. These days, she prefers a life away from the limelight but the beauty queen who made history and headlines around the world says, "I will always be an unofficial ambassador for South Africa."

In 1994 apartheid officially came to an end when F.W. de Clerk's government repealed the Population Registration Act, and the first multi-racial democratic elections were held, resulting in a coalition government with a non-white majority.

Bopthuthatswana, Transkei and the remaining homelands were reintegrated into South Africa.

Following Jacqui Mofokeng's stunning victory in 1993, the next six winners of Miss South Africa were either black or mixed race. But it was the story of the 1996 titleholder, Peggy-Sue Khumalo, which encapsulated the changes within South Africa better than any other before or since.

Born into rural KwaZulu Natal, Peggy-Sue was raised by a mother who, denied an education under apartheid, worked as a maid all her life. But she was determined that her daughter Peggy-Sue would have a better chance in life, and any spare money was spent on her education.

In 1990, the year Peggy-Sue finished high school, Nelson Mandela was released from prison after years of captivity, but changes in South Africa were slow to happen, and she found it hard to accept that her dream of becoming a lawyer was impossible due to lack of money. Trapped in a series of menial jobs, Peggy-Sue searched for a way out. This came in the form of a local beauty pageant, offering furniture as its first prize.

"My mum wasn't allowed time off to go and watch me, and I became even more driven: I've got to win this, I've got to get my mum out of this environment, where people can dictate what she can and cannot do."

That determination paid off, and she won the contest, which qualified her for the final of Miss South Africa. "I couldn't afford to lose," she told the BBC, "I thought this is my moment now – nobody is going to take it away."

In one extraordinary night, she not only won the Miss South Africa title, but immediately afterwards received a call from Nelson Mandela, inviting her and her mother to visit him in Pretoria the next day. During that meeting, he told Peggy-Sue that if he could do anything to help make her reign a success, to let him know.

She knew immediately what she wanted – "It wasn't my plan to pop champagne bottles, cut ribbons, look pretty and find a rich man" – and she asked the President to help her find a way into higher education.

President Mandela, a man known to be passionate about education, arranged for Investec Investment Bank to sponsor Peggy-Sue's university fees and, upon his recommendation, she moved to England and took up a position at Manchester University. Upon graduating in Economics in 2004, she became an investment banker in the City of

London before returning home in 2007. "We must all give back to South Africa," she said.

She is now head of public sector business at Investec – the very bank that sponsored her further education – and works with a number of charities for children from rural areas and those with intellectual disabilities.

"Tata Madiba" – Nelson Mandela – "remains my inspiration," she said. "He taught me that, in every interaction, everyone is equal."

The Miss World Organisation's *Beauty With a Purpose* fundraising arm raised money for the Nelson Mandela Foundation in Africa and the man himself delivered a message, via his grandson, Chief Mandela, to the 2011 final expressing his thanks and support.

From Penelope Coelen in 1958, to Anneline Kriel in 1974, South Africa had to wait a long forty years before the Miss World crown returned once more to their land.

In the London ExCel Centre, 22-year-old student doctor Rolene Strauss took the title in 2014, having been the favourite from the start. The fact that she was the third white South African to win the Miss World crown did not escape attention and debate in the South African media, yet a black columnist for the South African *Times* chided those who attempted to play the race card.

"I do not see what race has to do with her victory", she said. "We need to move beyond colour and treat every South African as equals."

Rolene herself was very aware of her position and responsibility, as the first post-apartheid South African Miss World. "We are celebrating twenty years of democracy this year," she told reporters. "We are an example to the rest of the world."

South Africa had travelled a long, rocky and tragic road since the National Party introduced apartheid in 1948, to its conclusion in 1994 with the first multi-racial democratic elections. The Miss World pageant reflected its political landscape in so many ways.

In a country still divided, the final word belongs to the late, great Nelson Mandela, whose inspiration lives on:

"No one is born hating another person because of the colour of his skin, or his background, or his religion. People must learn to hate, and if they can learn to hate, they can be taught to love, for love comes more naturally to the human heart than its opposite."

Sheena Monnin, Miss Pennsylvania USA 2012

"The organisation is fraudulent, inconsistent and trashy"

Accusations of fixing in the pageant world are nothing new; indeed they are part of beauty queen folklore.

Rare is the pageant that passes without some sort of muttering of rigging: the winner knowing the judges too well, the organisers arranging who has won beforehand to gain maximum publicity for their company or sponsors; even of backhanders changing hands to ensure the 'right' contestant wins.

Yet few disgruntled onlookers would expect to end up $5m poorer as a result of their complaint, as was the fate that befell Sheena Monnin, Miss Pennsylvania USA 2012.

On her official profile on the Miss USA website, the Psychology graduate spoke enthusiastically of her happiness at being part of the pageant.

"Being a Miss USA contestant has been the greatest journey of my life! Each day leading to Miss USA is filled with breathtaking anticipation, beautiful moments, incredible opportunities...and LOTS of excitement!"

A few days after the Miss USA 2012 pageant, the joy and excitement appeared to have waned, and Sheena Monnin accused the Miss Universe Organisation – headed at that time by Donald Trump – of out-and-out cheating.

She wrote a damning post on her Facebook page, alleging that the Top 5 had been chosen in advance of the live show.

"I witnessed another contestant - who said she saw the list of the Top 5 BEFORE THE SHOW EVER STARTED – then proceed to call out in order the Top 5 before they were announced on stage," the indignant beauty queen wrote. "After indeed it was the Top 5 I knew the show must be rigged; I decided at that moment to distance myself from an organisation which did not allow fair play and whose morals did not match my own."

She was, she went on, resigning as Miss Pennsylvania USA.

"Effective immediately, I have voluntarily, completely, and utterly removed myself from the Miss Universe Organisation.

"In good conscience I can no longer be affiliated in any way with an organisation I consider fraudulent, lacking in morals, inconsistent and in many ways, trashy."

Pageant officials were quick to dismiss Sheena's claims as false and in doing so asserted that she was resigning for a very different reason.

They believed that 27-year-old Sheena took offence to the fact that, for the first time in its history, transgender contestants were allowed to compete in the Miss Universe pageant system.

As detailed in *More Misdemeanours*, Canadian Jenna Talackova was born a boy, but by the age of 19 her gender transition was complete and she began modelling and competing in pageants.

However, the Miss Universe Canada organisation disqualified her on the grounds that she was not a "naturally-born female" – as required in their rules and regulations. Jenna fought back and sued Donald Trump to force his organisation to reverse his decision.

After a protracted battle played out in the media, Trump backed down and ruled that transgender women would be allowed to compete in his pageants. Not everyone was happy with this decision, though – including Miss Pennsylvania USA, Sheena Monnin,

When she resigned, following what she considered was a rigged Miss USA pageant, officials released an email to them that she had sent the following day. It read:

"I refuse to be part of a pageant system that has so far and so completely removed itself from its foundational principles as to allow and support natural born males to compete in it. This goes against every moral fibre of my being."

The winner of Miss USA that night, Olivia Culpo, had voiced her support for transgender beauty queens during the final – and became the first woman from Rhode Island to take the crown in the 60-year history of the pageant.

The statement from the pageant officials went on to say that, "We are disappointed that Monnin would attempt to steal the spotlight from Olivia Culpo on her well-deserved Miss USA win. The contestant she privately sourced as her reference [of pageant fixing] has vehemently refuted her most recent claim."

Speaking on *Good Morning America* three days after the pageant, Donald Trump called Sheena's claims of fixing, "ridiculous", going on to explain that the judges' votes are all verified and supervised by accountancy giant Ernst & Young.

"There was no Top 5 as that's impossible, nobody has any idea who the judges would be voting for. The organisation doesn't care who the Top 5 or the Top 10 is – what difference does it make?

"It's really disgraceful that she has done this and what we've authorised today is that we're going to bring a lawsuit against this girl. The person who supposedly told her the list now totally denies it and said that there is no list, and that she's never seen a list."

The TV anchor then asked Trump if he had actually met Sheena Monnin, and what his impressions of her were.

Trump replied, "I saw her there, and my impressions were that she didn't have a chance of being in the Top 15, not even close. All this is, is a girl who went there, lost, wasn't in the Top 15, and she's angry at the pageant system. We call that loser's remorse.

"She said some very strong things. She's using the word 'fraud' — that's pretty strong. So we're going to be suing her on that basis."

Hours later, Trump indicated that he would not seek legal action after all, on the condition that Sheena apologised immediately.

Trump's Special Counsel, Michael Cohen, called in live to *TMZ News*, and stated, "Donald Trump believes in giving everyone a second chance, including Ms Sheena Monnin.

"Accordingly, if Ms Monnin, in writing received by Mr Trump within the next 24 hours, apologises and withdraws her utterly baseless claim that the Miss USA pageant results were predetermined, then and only then will Mr Trump and the Miss USA Organisation not proceed with litigation against Ms Monnin seeking massive damages for her defamatory and offensive remarks.

"There are many things that Ms Monnin could've done to enhance her career; this was not a smart choice."

Sheena resolutely refused to accept the ultimatum to apologise and, 48 hours later, appeared on *The Today Show* sofa. Asked how she felt about Trump's proposed lawsuit, she replied, "I'm disappointed at some of the statements Trump has made about me, and I feel prepared to continue to pursue the truth. I know what I heard, and I know what I in turn witnessed. What I want out of this is for the truth to be known."

Miss Florida USA, Karina Brez, was alleged to have been the source of the information about the Top 5 list and, just before Sheena's interview on *The Today Show*, issued a full denial.

"I want to make a statement, very firmly and very clearly, that I did not at any time tell Miss Pennsylvania USA or other Miss USA contestants that I knew the final five contestants in the pageant," Brez wrote.

"For reasons I don't understand, my name is now being brought forward as the person who released the names and implied that the Final 5 contestants were pre-selected. This is absolutely not true, and not the case.

"Backstage during the pageant, I did see a piece of paper with names on it, and like most people in such frenetic circumstances, joked that they must be the names of the final contestants. It was a throwaway comment, in the stress of the pageant, and was never meant as a fact. The list I saw didn't even have the eventual winner on it.

"Since this situation arose, and accusations made, I have spoken with pageant officials and with Mr Trump's representatives. I have told them what happened, and that there was never any malicious implication made in my jocular statements. Miss Pennsylvania USA is using this situation for her own ends. I want it firmly understood that I am honored and privileged to serve as Miss Florida USA and to have competed in the Miss USA pageant. I would never do anything to undermine the Pageant in any way."

When asked on *The Today Show* if Sheena may have misinterpreted what Karina had implied, she was adamant that that wasn't the case.

"I have many years of psychological training," she said. "I know when someone is scared and serious. Her body language was serious.

"After the Top 16 had been announced and we were backstage, she said that she had seen the list with the names of the Top 5. She said, 'I know who the Top 5 are going to be'. I told her to wait and see who the Top 5 were, as maybe it was a rehearsals list she had seen. But when the names were called out in the order that she said she saw them on this list, that's just too coincidental to not be true.

"I feel an injustice has been done, not only to the other people who were not in the Top 5, but to the thousands of pageant girls across the nation who compete, believing this pageant is an honest system, as I did for nine years."

Yet gossip website *TMZ* revealed that pageant sources had told them that Miss Florida had seen only one name of the eventual Top 5 finalists which, if true, would put added pressure on Sheena Monnin to substantiate her claims.

It seemed she had little support from any quarter. Two of the celebrity judges at the Miss USA final, Joe Jonas and Rob Kardashian, made statements on Twitter in support of the Miss Universe Organisation, while Ernst & Young, the accounting firm in charge of verification of the voting, said:

"Neither the Miss Universe Organization, Donald Trump, NBC, the eight celebrity judges, nor any of the contestants could have known who the final five Miss USA finalists were before the evening gown competition was completed and the tabulation was verified by Ernst & Young during the live broadcast."

But ten days after the furore first blew up, Sheena found unexpected support from an anonymous source.

One of her fellow Miss USA contestants came forward and spoke to gossip supremo Perez Hilton, on the proviso that she wasn't named.

"I saw Florida backstage and she was very, very flustered and upset," the contestant told Hilton. "At that point she was able to reveal to me at least four of the five names who went on to be the top girls. She couldn't remember the fifth because she was so upset. Several of the girls then started hearing through the grapevine about a list; a lot of people were upset."

Hilton was dismissive of these claims. "Sheena Monnin is going to need all the help she can get to continue her quest for the truth, as well as defend herself against a defamation lawsuit," he said on his website. "We don't think the support of an anonymous contestant is going to cut it either."

A former judge at the Miss Universe pageant also had a view which may well have given Sheena's allegations some credence.

Richard Johnson, journalist at *The New York Post* and editor of the *Page Six* gossip column, wrote of his experience as a judge under Trump's watchful eye.

"Just in case a judge was indecisive," he wrote, "Trump was sitting right behind us in the front row, close enough to chat with us during commercial breaks, letting us know his preferences. Was he just making small talk, or trying to influence our votes? Did his voice carry more weight than any other fan who was applauding and shouting for their favourite? Probably.

"But the pageant wasn't rigged. I voted for the contestant I thought was the most beautiful. Most of the time, Trump and I agreed. But not every time."

Less than a week since Sheena's statement and, in the light of her refusal to apologise, the Miss Universe Organisation filed two claims against her: one for defamation, the other for breach of contract, and in doing so seeking "significant damages".

A stipulation in Sheena Monnin's Miss Pennsylvania contract required any dispute to be handled through private arbitration first, only progressing to court should a resolution not be found.

On 18th December 2012, a district court judge in New York ruled that "the method in which the Miss USA pageant is judged...precludes any reasonable possibility that the judging was rigged".

The judge awarded $5m in damages to the Miss Universe Organisation, to be paid by Sheena Monnin. The sum was calculated as a result of a potential sponsor for the 2013 pageant pulling out in the light of Sheena's allegations.

After the ruling, Trump called Monnin's actions "disgraceful" and said, "We cannot allow a disgruntled contestant to make false and reckless statements which are damaging to the many people who have devoted their hearts and souls to the Miss Universe, Miss USA and Miss Teen USA pageant systems.

"She was angry that she lost, she went on *The Today Show* and she said really bad stuff. You can't rig the celebrity judges. Ernst & Young tabulate the results, and they were unbelievably upset about her comments.

"Going to arbitration was the appropriate action to take under the circumstances, and while I feel very badly for Sheena, she did the wrong thing. She was really nasty, and we had no choice. It is an expensive lesson for her."

Sheena told the *Pittsburgh Tribunal-Review* that she was "shocked" at the ruling, adding that, "The most logical course of action is to fight the decision".

She also highlighted a clause in the Miss USA contract which states that the Miss Universe Organisation, Donald Trump, and others have the legal right to choose the top five and the winner, irrespective of any publicised selection process.

"They're saying that it's a blatant disregard of the truth, but the truth is right here in the contract," Sheena told the newspaper.

Michael Cohen, Trump's attorney, admitted the clause existed. "It's protection for the Miss Universe pageant and its owners," he told the New York Daily News. "It has never been used. The judges' decision has never been overruled."

Sheena took the case to the Court of Appeal, but on 2nd July 2013, the Southern District Court of New York upheld the ruling and ordered her to pay the £5m to Trump's organisation.

In his ruling, the Judge said, "The Court does not take lightly that Monnin is compelled to pay what is a devastating monetary award. However, sympathy, or apparent inequity, may play no role in a court's legal analysis."

"I was hoping for a different outcome," Sheena said afterwards, with masterful understatement, "but am pleased that the true nature of the Miss USA judging procedure has been exposed."

She claimed that testimony for the organisation revealed the pageant selects the top 15 contestants, "irrespective of the preliminary judges' scores."

"This is not about me being a 'sore loser' or wanting my 15 minutes of fame," Monnin wrote in a statement on her Facebook page. "This is about the MUO's admission under oath that they manipulate the judges' results to suit their own ends. This is not what they advertise to the public."

Michael Cohen said he was "astounded" by her latest remarks. "I respectfully disagree with every statement made by Ms Monnin in her most recent posting. One would think she would be very mindful of any future comments in light of this most recent decision."

Sheena appealed for contributions towards her $50,000 legal bill on Facebook and on the Sheena Monnin Legal Defense Fund website.

Faced with a vast debt to Trump and, with no feasible way of paying it, she was forced to agree with the Judge's proclamation that Sheena was "undeniably suffering from a poor choice of counsel, who chose to ignore the responsibilities owed to his client".

In fact, she agreed with the Judge so much that she sued her counsel, Richard Klineburger III, for malpractice, and won a pay-out of £1m.

Trump agreed to settle with her for this sum, and the case was closed.

The winner of that much-debated Miss USA pageant, Olivia Culpo, went on to become the first American to win the Miss Universe crown in 15 years – a result that, unsurprisingly, was accepted by all.

Yet Olivia's reign was not without controversy. In October 2013, she was blasted for posing in front of the Taj Mahal in high heels, as part of a photoshoot.

The Archaeological Society of India lodged a complaint against her and her agency, accusing her of violating strict product placement rules at the monument, and calling her actions "inappropriate".

The incident took place at the marble bench popularly known as the Diana Seat, in tribute to the Princess of Wales's iconic photograph at that spot in 1992.

The Archaeological Society claimed that "high heels of a particular brand were taken out of a bag by someone in the group. Olivia Culpo donned one of the sandals and held another in her hand, reportedly to advertise them while her cameramen shot the scene, with the Taj Mahal in the background."

Olivia, who also stood on top the Diana Seat to pose, was looking at a two-year prison sentence and fine of $1,600 if found guilty.

But the 21 year old was adamant that she had never wanted to do the shoot.

She told the *Providence Journal*, "Honestly, I did say out loud at one point, 'Isn't this a little inappropriate?' I was given directions to pose with the shoes and, honestly, five-inch heels on a ten-inch bench in 90-degree weather – you know, I didn't want to do it."

The Miss Universe Organisation stepped in to apologise, and explained that the footage was to form part of Olivia's video diary of her year's reign.

"The filming that took place outside the Taj Mahal was never intended to be used as a commercial nor was it meant in any way to be disrespectful," their statement said. "We sincerely apologize for any unintentional harm our indiscretion and insensitivity may have caused."

Olivia dated singer Nick Jonas – brother of Miss USA judge Joe – for two years, and they quickly established themselves as media favourites. They split up in 2015 but Olivia continues to be in demand as TV presenter and anchor woman at high profile events such as *The Emmys*.

Sheena Monin gave an exclusive interview with *The Guardian* in 2016. She said that her objection to transgender contestants had been taken out of context, and that her upset had been over the rules being suddenly changed without notice. "The point I was trying to make – and I don't think I made it well – is that they changed the contract and I don't think that's fair."

Her Facebook post, in which she set out her reasons for resigning, was never meant to be seen by the wider world, she said, but Trump spotted it and escalated the conflict out of all context.

Trump's lawsuit knocked her for six. "There's no way I could've afforded to pay that off and frankly he had to have known that," she said. "I was just a normal person."

She spent three years battling Trump and his lawyers, a period she described as the most traumatic of her life. "Every day seemed to bring a new legal document that I didn't understand, that I had to seek legal counsel on."

Sheena rebuffed the notion that Trump had ruined her life, but had succeeded in making her feel small and afraid, and very much used by the organization as an example. "There was this message being sent out to all the contestants: you better not say anything bad about us."

In an interview in *GQ* magazine in 2016, pageant coach Jeff Lee revealed that Trump would handpick as many as six Miss Universe finalists – 'Trump cards', as they were called – allegedly in response to his own personal favourite from Ukraine not making the cut in 2014.

Lee believes this is why so many eastern European contestants made the semi-finals during Trump's tenure, but stressed that he didn't pick mere clones of his wife Melania – "He liked India a lot, too".

Sheena Monin's self-help book, *Hands on the Wheel: Getting Control of Your Life,* was published in 2016 and drew on her experiences at the hands of Trump, with advice for readers on the best way to deal with bullies.

As for the concept of her former boss becoming President of the US, she said, "If you have someone who goes after me, a normal person, when all I did was write on Facebook something he disagreed with, then what would happen if you had a real grievance against him and you started speaking out."

The world, like Sheena herself, is just starting to find out.

The Battles and Victories of Miss Israel

"Inside I was screaming, 'Help me! Save me! I'm about to die!"
Linor Abargil, Miss World 1998

Israel, a state created in 1948, is only 69 years old, yet the Miss Israel pageant has run, uninterrupted, for 66 of those years, an extraordinary statistic for a nation that has constantly battled unrest, tragedy and war.

The pageant was created by publisher and author, the late Hemda Nofech-Mozes, who married into Israel's most powerful media family. She founded *La'Isha* magazine for women a year before the nation's war of independence in 1948 and began the Miss Israel contest two years later.

"Everyone was talking about war," she said. "Everyone was talking about settlement. I said, wait a minute – there is a nation here, there are beautiful women."

As seen in a previous chapter, the presence of Israel in international pageants has caused more than its fair share of controversy, resentment and security scares, yet for a decade it was one of the most successful nations in both Miss Universe and Miss World.

Between 1964 and 1976, Israel only twice failed to make the semi-final in Miss Universe, while over at Miss World, their contestant made the top four in six years out of eight (between 1967 and 1974).

The fact that Israel has only won each title once can possibly be attributed to the security headaches that such a victory and, more to the point, year of office, would bring the organisers.

Yet the choice of Miss Israel winner so often reflected the changing faces of both Israeli and international society.

In 1952, during unrest between Israel's European veterans and Middle-Eastern Jewish newcomers, Yemen-born Ora Vered became the first winner of Middle-Eastern Jewish origin. When immigrants from the newly-liberated Soviet Union started to make their homes in Israel and across Europe in 1993, the title went to Jana Khodriker from the Ukraine.

Similarly in 1999, at a time when the country was at its most hopeful of peace between the Arabs and Israelis, Rana Raslan made history when she was crowned the first Arab winner of the Miss Israel pageant.

Yet almost inevitably, her victory was greeted with mixed voices, with some claiming her win was a purely political statement.

"It does not matter if I am Jewish or Arab," she said immediately after her crowning. "I will represent Israel the best that I can. We must live here in coexistence".

The Miss Israel pageant organiser was furious at suggestions that Rana won only because she was an Arab. "There will always be people who need to say something, anything," she fumed. "Rana won because she is beautiful and delicate and interesting – not because she is an Arab."

Arab politicians accused Israelis of using her victory as a cover for the discrimination that keeps many of the Arab minority – which in 1999 made up one-sixth of the six million population – below the poverty line.

"This is trivial equality," said one. "I hope she tells the world that she belongs to the weak sector that suffers from discrimination."

Human rights groups had long since campaigned for better property and employment rights for Israeli-Arabs, with living standards seen as far below those of Jewish people. Most Israeli Arabs lived under military rule until 1966, but even after curfews lifted, economic standards did not improve for them.

Israeli writer Irit Linor said she wasn't impressed that the "Arab sector had joined in this ridiculous celebration. How will an Arab girl in a swimsuit talking at the Miss World contest about closing the hole in the ozone layer help the Arab feminist cause, their status?"

Muslim fundamentalists called her 'immoral' for taking part in the swimsuit round, while Arab politicians claimed that Israel was using her to divert attention from what they perceived to be negative treatment of the Arab people by Israel.

Jewish Israelis weren't happy either, accusing Rana of not being the right person to represent a Jewish state – with a poll among their community showing that 64% said she did not represent them.

"It's shameful," said one, "Can't she be a beauty queen of another country?"

Yet Prime Minister Benjamin Netanyahu was thrilled at what he saw as a sign of Israel's progress. "This is a clear expression of equality and coexistence between Arabs and Jews in Israel," he said.

Other politicians weren't quite as optimistic as their leader. "It gave us a warm feeling," said Israeli parliament member Taleb a-Sanaa, an Arab. "But to say this is a revolution is going a bit overboard."

Yet she proved the toast of New York when she was flown to the USA for the anniversary celebration of The Abraham Fund, an organisation promoting Jewish-Arab relations in Israel.

Rana later admitted that she hadn't given the thorny issue of Jewish-Arab relations much thought, having grown up in Haifa, a city of mixed population.

Rana's parents divorced when she was 13 and she was brought up by her mother, who worked as a cook and cleaner to help ends meet, with her three siblings. Her oldest brother was jailed for assault when Rana was 15.

Despite entering smaller beauty pageants and embarking on a modelling career, she was reluctant to compete for the Miss Israel title because, in her mother's words, "they always pick Jews, never Arabs".

Rana's photo was chosen from 800 entries for the national final. "I couldn't believe it when they called out my name as the winner," she said.

Any anger she felt at the condemnation that greeted her – "because I felt they should've been proud of what I had achieved" - soon dissolved, in order to try and understand and "respect each person for their own ideas."

Yet such open-minded ideals were tested to the limit when she travelled to Trinidad & Tobago for the Miss Universe pageant.

She told reporters that she felt she was being ostracised by judges and fellow contestants for representing the Jewish state. Miss Lebanon, Rana said, had been forbidden to speak to her while Miss Egypt had allegedly called her "an Israeli collaborator".

She also said that she had been cold-shouldered by some of the judges, due to her choice of her blue and white dress decorated with a sequinned Jewish star. "One of them really wouldn't look at me," she told reporters.

Miss Guam had already been sent home from the pageant when it was discovered she was pregnant, while a local Muslim leader in Trinidad denounced the contest as projecting "lewdness, nudity, carnality and the intermingling of the sexes."

Rana married a millionaire Arab businessman in 2003 and now lives with him in Monte Carlo, London and Dubai. She appeared on Israel's version of *Celebrity Masterchef* in 2014.

Linor Abargil became one of the best known Israeli beauty queens, not as a result of any political incident or diplomatic row, but due to her own horrifying yet ultimately inspirational story.

The Miss World pageant returned to terrestrial TV for the first time in ten years in 1998, courtesy of a three-year deal with Channel Five, which beat off bids from two other broadcasters to screen the event.

Channel Five promised to 'refresh' the format, and that first contest gave the channel its highest viewing figure in its short history, with 3.2m tuning in at peak time. Singer Ronan Keating hosted a lavish final in the Seychelles, with celebrity judges including rugby star Jonah Lomu and racing driver Jacques Villeneuve.

Linor Abargil entered the Miss Israel contest purely because the prizes included a new car and trip to Thailand, yet she went on to become the first ever Israeli winner of Miss World, and the Channel Five event was judged to be an unqualified success.

But what the viewing public didn't know is that Linor's tears were less of joy, than of shock and confusion over a violent attack she had suffered just weeks before the pageant.

Six weeks beforehand, the 18 year old had been modelling in Milan, yet wasn't happy there and was keen to return home. Her modelling agency gave her the details of a Hebrew-speaking travel agent, Egyptian-born Uri Shlomo, with whom they had worked for many years, and whom they said she could trust.

"He looked like a nice, professional man," Linor recalled. "He showed me that there were no flights to Israel, but he promised to help me."

Shlomo told Linor he had managed to find a flight departing from Rome, and that he would drive her there.

"Later, I realised that this act was carefully planned, and that I wasn't the first who would be harmed by him," she said. "I was very naïve. You don't think people can do such a bad thing to others, especially when you're 18.

"The vision of this terrible night, 6th October 1998, would visit my nightmares for many years. He took a secluded road, telling me that avoiding the freeway would save me the tolls. He had brought a knife, a rope, and a plastic bag. There was no flight from Rome, no ticket. He never planned that I would leave.

"I was tied up, stabbed, strangled, gagged, and repeatedly raped. There finally came a moment when I was able to start talking with him, and a survival instinct took over.

"I told him: 'It's a one-night stand'. I had heard this in a movie once and thought it was a good line. He was telling me all the time that he was sorry and that I couldn't tell anyone and I had to promise to him that I would tell no-one.

"I asked him about his family and he told me he had a son. I tried to get through to him. He suddenly snapped out of it. He admitted that we had never left Milan. He had driven around in circles."

When she rang her mother immediately after the attack, she urged her daughter not to take a shower, and that she needed to go to the police and get a medical examination.

Italian police negligence allowed Shlomo - later discovered to be a serial rapist - to walk free due to lack of immediate evidence but, once back in Israel, the authorities there issued an arrest warrant. He was tricked into returning to Israel, subjected to a lengthy trial, and finally sentenced to sixteen years in prison, securing his conviction by DNA found in his car.

When Linor was competing at Miss World in the Seychelles, the police were in the midst of their investigation.

"My mum thought going to Miss World would help take my mind off the rape, but I was just going through the motions. Inside I was screaming, 'Help me! Save me! I'm about to die!' Nobody there knew what I had been through.

"I was in the Seychelles, I was with great girls. I didn't care about the competition, I just wanted to forget. I didn't think I had a chance of winning – Israel never won. I just wanted to go home. Then I heard from a distance: 'The winner is Miss Israel'.

"When I stood on stage with the crown on my head, I think it was the first time that I realised what had happened to me three months ago - and that I needed to go home immediately," Linor told the *Daily Telegraph* in an interview in 2014.

"I couldn't stay there for another minute. Going from the extreme of almost dying to being on that huge stage, with millions of people watching, was too much."

After the contest, Linor spoke to organisers Eric and Julia Morley and told them about her ordeal, explaining that her travels as Miss World may be curtailed due to her having to be available to the Israeli police to give evidence against Shmolo.

"They were very understanding," she said. "They only made me do some of the media interviews.

"When I returned home, the whole city was waiting on the streets to greet me. I was a hero. But I wasn't able to fulfil my duties. I couldn't go to events and smile and wave."

Days after 43-year-old Shlomo had been detained, and a month after her Miss World win, Linor's story – initially subject to a gagging order so as not to alert Shlomo to the fact that he was being sought - was released to the media, and suddenly she was in every newspaper in the world.

She was speaking out, she said, to encourage other rape victims to have the courage to do so, but wanted details of the case withheld until her attacker had been held.

When asked by a journalist if she thought that the Miss World organisation had been aware of the rumours of her attack and given her the title out of sympathy, she disagreed. "I won the title in my own right," she said, "and not as a result of charity.

"Women who are assaulted must react to the crimes committed against them," she said in her statement, "even at the price of some public exposure, so that these incidents do not become an accepted, routine part of our lives.

"From the moment I was crowned Miss World, I knew it was my destiny to encourage other women to speak out. People always laugh at Miss Worlds because they want to save the planet and because they wave nicely. I really believe that the people who get power in the world should try to change the world – even if it's by changing one woman."

Her courage to speak out was hailed by women's groups in Israel and worldwide.

When Linor crowned Rana Raslan as her successor in the Miss Israel pageant a year later, she gave a defiant speech at the end of the telecast about the violent rape she had suffered at the hands of her travel agent the year before, and her campaign to provide victims with a voice.

"I've been through a lot this year. Thank you to all of you at home for all the love you gave me. To all of those who relate to beauty contests as meat markets: you should know, we do with our bodies what we want. Only what *we* want, and no one else."

Sixteen years after the attack Linor, by this time a mother of three and a qualified lawyer, unveiled her documentary, *Brave Miss World*, at the Jewish Film Festival.

Telling the story of her attack and subsequent activism to encourage women to speak out, the film – which had been funded by grants, investors and donations - saw her interviewing dozens of other women from all over the world who had survived rape, including Joan Collins.

The legendary actress gave an emotional interview to Linor on camera, recalling how her virginity was taken at the age of 17, after she was given the date-rape drug Rohypnol, by Hollywood actor Maxwell Reed.

"And anyway the bottom line is that he called me," Joan told Linor, "and I went out with him again. And after I'd been going out with him for a few months, he asked me to marry him. And I thought, 'Well I better because you know, he took my virginity.'

"I really hated him, but I was so filled with guilt, that he had done this thing to me. It took a long time to be able to really trust any man."

Linor was exceptionally moved by Joan's honesty.

"It was very emotional to hear how Joan had felt so guilty about losing her virginity to this older man who had drugged and raped her, that she felt she had to marry him," she said.

"When she found out about the film, she decided she would help us. It's not something any of us want to do - to go on camera and talk about having been raped. But when you know that speaking up can give others the courage to come forward and press charges, and how many others will be saved by putting a rapist in prison, you want to do it."

The director of the documentary Cecilia Peck (daughter of actor Gregory) acknowledged the toll that filming took on Linor.

"Linor thought she was ready, but discovered that telling her story and listening to the stories of the other women triggered her own trauma over and over again," she said.

"There were days that were very hard. There were months where Linor had to shut down filming and couldn't go on. It was absolutely heartbreaking to hear every story, but every one of the women who spoke up in the film told us at the time, and have since, how much it helped their healing process to know that what happened to them could help someone else to feel they're not alone.

"We visited very young girls at the Teddy Bear Clinic in Soweto. They could not believe that a Miss World was in their tiny clinic listening to them. And they said, 'People just tell us, you cry too much'.

"And Linor said to them, 'You know what you tell them? Say, yes. And if you don't give me support, I'll cry louder.' And she embraced them. And she left those girls saying, 'I know that you're in turn going to help other girls.'"

Linor said that she herself was in therapy for two years to help her deal with her attack, and that making the documentary, which was subsequently released on internet streaming channel Netflix, and hearing the stories of others was her "personal journey of acceptance."

"At the time of my winning Miss World, I wanted to die, basically. I didn't even care really. But God had different plans. I guess this crown was for me to do what I'm doing today. I'm travelling around the world and meeting amazing groups of men and women. As all Miss Worlds say, I wanted to save the world.

"Well, I took it seriously.

"I think it's very important to speak up. Because these women who don't speak, they don't want to believe it's happened. They're afraid to mention the word rape.

"If they say the word 'rape' they can shake all over and faint. It controls you. And for what? You let this person control you for the rest of your life. I think when you put what happened to you on the side, and you're not afraid to confront it, then you realise it's not what makes you who you are."

Linor realised that she found it easier to speak out than others: "I wasn't like the other girls. I never blamed myself, or thought it happened because of me. I never kept it inside."

"At the time what I did felt normal. But now I realise that it wasn't. Because most victims don't speak, ever. I'm quite unique in that way. I speak, I shout, I'm not afraid."

"I want to bring the subject of rape out of the shadows and into the light."

The documentary was nominated for an Emmy award in the Exceptional Merit in Documentary Filmmaking, and the resulting *#IAmBrave* Educational Screening Campaign, to stimulate conversation and awareness of the issues raised in the film, continues around the world to this day.

The *Brave Miss World* website, offering resources and a forum for survivors of rape, has received over 85 million hits.

Linor's first marriage to a Lithuanian basketball player in 2006 ended in divorce two years later. In 2010 she married Oren Halfon, with whom she had three children, including a set of twins. Linor qualified as a lawyer and is now an advocate in the fight against sexual violence.

Uri Shlomo was released from prison in January 2015, having served a 16-year sentence.

"The real healing," said Linor, "is in the heart, and the real victory is to go back and discover your trusting, believing self – the self who can trust somebody else, and who is capable of giving and of receiving."

When Yityish Aynaw was crowned the first black Miss Israel in 2013, her victory signalled what was hoped would be a new chapter in race relations in her country.

An estimated 125,000 Ethiopians had settled in Israel over the past thirty years as a result of a government programme to relocate Ethiopian Jews who faced persecution in their homeland. The Ethiopian Jewish community was airlifted to the safety of the Jewish state in a series of audacious and covert rescue operations beginning in 1984.

In 2011, it was claimed that Israel had achieved the remarkable feat of transporting Ethiopia's entire 2000-year-old Jewish community – known as Beta Israel - to a new life, where they would theoretically be provided with a safe haven from the famine, political unrest and civil wars of their land of birth.

Yet accusations of racism against Israel's Ethiopian population have long been levelled at the government, with those living in segregated communities complaining of being denied jobs and housing, their children refused places at local schools, and of indiscriminate targeting by the police.

Israel's health ministry refused to deny reports in 2012 that many of the newly-arrived Ethiopian women had been injected with a contraceptive without their full consent, resulting in the birth rate of Israel's Ethiopian population decreasing by fifty percent, while the rest of the population saw an increase.

Another sign of Israel's failure to absorb the newcomers was the revelation in the 1990s that the Israeli national blood bank had routinely destroyed blood donated by Ethiopian Israelis for fear of HIV, while landlords in southern Israel had allegedly agreed not to rent or sell their property to Jews of Ethiopian origin.

This widespread and ongoing prejudice and persecution resulted in thousands joining anti-racism rallies in Jerusalem in 2012 to protest against the treatment of the Beta Israel community.

It was therefore tempting for the more cynical commentators to see Yityish Aynaw's crowning as the first Ethiopian-born Miss Israel a year later as a very well-timed victory for human rights. Yet her Cinderella story touched the hearts of everyone who tuned in – over a quarter of Israeli TV viewers - to see her take the crown.

Born in a small township in north-west Ethiopia, Yityish – known as Titi – lost her father to undisclosed means a year after she was born, and a decade later her mother died from a sudden illness. At the age of 12, she was sent with her younger brother to Israel to live with her maternal grandparents, who had moved there in 2000.

Jews in Ethiopia grew up dreaming of moving to Israel. "I was told that this was the land of milk and honey," she told *Tablet* magazine, "That I'd go out on the street, bend down and pick up golden coins. I'd turn on the tap and milk would pour out."

"The journey was, I think, what saved me," she says. "Because I was deeply hurt and I wanted to escape from Ethiopia and forget everything that had happened and get on with it," she adds. "I wanted to break away from everything and go on."

While still a child, Titi was suddenly faced with a new language, a new culture and the challenges that came with starting a new life in a foreign country.

She and brother were taken by their grandparents to live in the immigrant neighbourhood of Netanya, where they were promptly sent off to boarding school in Haifa, not knowing one word of the Hebrew language.

"It wasn't easy because I couldn't speak the language and I was put into a normal class without any help," she told the BBC World Service. "They threw me into deep water, but that's how you learn to swim the best."

"It was a new language. It was a new culture. Quite often children even laughed at me," she says, though she also made many friends and proved a popular classmate. "If you feel like you're going to be segregated, then you will be segregated, but if you feel like you're going to be part of society then you're accepted."

But Titi was determined to succeed in her adopted country.

"I felt a responsibility to prove myself in everything I did and to improve myself as well," she says.

Titi excelled at school, becoming school council president and winning a national student film competition with a short feature of an Ethiopian immigrant girl in Israel who tried to forget her heritage –

which, she says, was based on several of her classmates who were embarrassed to be reminded of where they were from.

Like all Israelis, Titi was required to serve in the army, and she rose to the rank of military police commander, in charge of ninety soldiers, teaching them how to fire a weapon, perform security checks and detect bombs.

After she left the army, Titi spent her savings on a flight to Addis Ababa in Ethiopia, in order to try to come to terms with the death of her mother, feelings she acknowledged that she had buried for too long.

"I never looked at her photos, I never talked about her. I decided to erase everything," she said. "It was a defence mechanism. I needed to succeed. I don't have parents that I can crash with until I'm a 40 year old."

Titi was shocked and upset at the condition of her mother's gravestone in the neglected Ethiopian cemetery, and paid the groundsman to completely refurbish the grave, staying in Addis Ababa until the work was complete.

When she returned home, she landed a job as a manager of a shoe shop and, shortly afterwards, got a phone call from a friend to say she had entered her into a heat of the Miss Israel contest.

"I refused to ever smile at soldiers while I was a lieutenant in case it compromised my authority," she said. "And suddenly I'm a beauty queen and I have to smile all the time!

"It's time that someone from my community, someone with my skin colour, who is Israeli just like everyone else, represented the country," she said. "I feel like I've made history, that I've blazed a trail."

The national director of the Miss Israel pageant said of Titi afterwards, "I think she was not the most beautiful, by classical standards. But she stands on the stage and you cannot ignore her."

There were, naturally, the detractors – those who said she won only because she was black; those calling her a "toffee queen" instead of a "yoffee" (Hebrew for 'beauty') queen; and those who taunted that her family couldn't have watched the pageant because they were too poor to own a television.

"Tell me I'm ugly, that would hurt less," Titi said.

Titi never tried to downplay the situation in her adopted homeland. "I'm not ashamed to say that there is racism in Israel," she admitted to the *BuzzFeed* newsite. "It's a problem, but a problem that Israel is trying to fix."

During her reign, she met President Obama – "my role model" – when White House officials invited her to his gala dinner during his state visit to Jerusalem.

After they had been introduced by the Israeli President Shimon Peres, Titi admitted she was overwhelmed. "He's an exciting man, a world-class hunk, charming and an extraordinary gentleman," she said. "It was an unreal feeling, the most beautiful and exciting moment of the past year."

"You are very beautiful," Obama told her, according to Israeli media. "And Michelle would be very happy to be as tall as you are."

Titi told *Tablet* magazine that to compete in a beauty pageant and tell the judges that you wished for world peace was 'stupid.'

"Iran is trying to develop a nuclear weapon, China is trying to become a superpower," she said. "To say that I want world peace, of course I want it. It's a dream. But I don't think it will happen now."

Despite being one of the hot favourites to win the Miss Universe pageant in Moscow, Titi was unplaced, but her determination to make a difference was undiminished.

She spoke of her plans to open a community centre for at-risk teenagers in her largely Ethiopian neighbourhood of Netanya, while harbouring a dream that her modelling career would take off to such an extent that she would be chosen for a *Victoria's Secrets* fashion show.

Her victory as Miss Israel, however, will go down in history.

"I think I won because it's not only about beauty. Beauty queen or not, it's about being yourself, believing in yourself and being special."

In 2012, the Israeli city of Haifi hosted the first ever Miss Holocaust Survivor pageant, in which women aged between 74 and 97 took to the red carpet to describe the horrors they suffered at the hands of the Nazis in World War Two, and to talk about their own contribution to the community.

Over 300 women applied, with 14 chosen for the final. The event was described as "macabre" by one Holocaust survivors' group, but defended by the organisers, the Helping Hand charity, as "meaningful".

"They feel good together," a spokesman said, "They are having a good time and laughing in rehearsals. The fact that so many wanted to participate shows that it's a good idea. They were stripped of their childhood and adolescence. This evening gives them the chance to transcend their trauma and have some fun."

The winner of Miss Holocaust Survivor was 79-year-old Hava Hershkovitz, who fled her native Romania in 1941, and was sent to a detention camp in the Soviet Union for three years.

"It's not easy at this age to be in a beauty contest," she said as she accepted the crown. "But we're all doing it to show we're still alive, that we're still here."

Scoring Drugs for Miss World 1961...and other stories

Jon Osborne
Former Director at Miss World Ltd

B ut for Eric and Julia Morley's demands, Miss World very nearly had a starring role in one of the biggest films of the 70s – *The Return of the Pink Panther*.

Peter Sellers had been a judge at the Miss World pageant in 1963, but it wasn't until ten years later that I met him on the set of the movie at Shepperton Film Studios for a meeting with the producer Blake Edwards, husband of Julie Andrews. Sellers was a consummate professional and could not have been more charming to me.

The reason I was there was due to the plot of the film: a heist was taking place at the same time as the British public was glued to the Miss World pageant on TV (hard to believe now that Miss World was the top-rated show of the year back then). The producer was unable to get permission from the BBC to use footage from the most recently televised final, so he wanted to recreate moments from the pageant to use in the movie in the most authentic way possible.

In exchange for a credit on the film, we would supply the crown and sash, those silly numbered wristbands, trophies, and even some of our beauties to parade on stage, one of whom would be crowned the pretend winner.

The day I spent at Shepperton was wasted, though, when the Morleys changed their minds about only wanting a credit and demanded a substantial fee instead in return for our assistance. Blake Edwards indicated that a fee would not be payable and instead chose to purchase the rights of highlights from the 1974 World Cup in which England were playing.

My weirdest encounter with a celebrity happened during a Miss England contest in the early 70s. The organisers and contestants all shared the same hotel, The Waldorf, and prior to the live final at the Lyceum the judges would meet with three contestants at a time for a brief interview.

Usually the judges at national pageants were British, but this year we were excited to obtain American heartthrob and star of *The Virginian* series, Doug McClure. The very personification of West Coast blond surfer boy, it was obvious to us that when we arrived for the interviews he was pretty spaced out.

McClure remained silently stoned for many of the interviews, until the next three contestants sat down. Among these ladies was one who had a nose resembling a ski slope. McClure leaned forward and asked her, "Tell me, when it rains and you don't have an umbrella, does the rain fall down your nose and shoot off into the air so the bottom of your face stays dry?"

Needless to say the room fell silent except for McClure's laughter. Eric Morley was horrified and tried to cover it as best as he could, but we were all worried about what could've been a very long night ahead with the stoned superstar.

My second rather unorthodox encounter with a celebrity judge happened when I woke early in my Glasgow hotel room on the day of the final of Miss Scotland to travel to the airport to collect judge Barbara Windsor. This *Carry On* actress was just as down to earth, friendly, bubbly and sexy and as her screen persona. When we got to the hotel, it was breakfast time so the doorman took her bags to her room and we went into the restaurant to dine.

By the end of that breakfast, she had kept me laughing, and had also divulged some of the most intimate details of her love life, especially her feelings for co-star (and married man) Sid James. A celebrity opening up to me in the way Miss Windsor did made me feel very special. I guess audiences today remember her best for her award winning role in *EastEnders*, but when she was chatting with me and making it seem I was privy to emotions she usually kept secret, I was most impressed to be in the company of a Tony-nominated super talent for her performance on Broadway in 1965 in *Oh What A Lovely War*.

Compare Miss Windsor's non-stop chat with the seven words directed to me by someone who, like me, was born and raised in South Carolina. Upon being introduced as such to legendary soul singer Eartha Kitt, she looked me up and down and said, "And did YOUR daddy own a plantation?" – before swivelling round on her bar stool away from me.

Miss United Kingdom 1975 produced another embarrassing moment from a judge. At the formal dinner on the night prior to the televised final, the Morleys were surrounded on the head table by the judges, who this year were Alvin Stardust, Rita Tushingham, Jack Hedley and Dora Bryan.

When Eric Morley addressed the guests and announced that this year was one of the strongest groups of entrants ever to participate, Miss Bryan interrupted to shout out, "My favourite is that cute little Miss Dundee!"

I challenge anyone who has ever been involved with pageants to tell me of a similar experience where a judge lets her choice be known 24 hours prior to the final in such a public way, in front of all the contestants. Morley tried to make light of the awkwardness of this situation and many of us were telling the contestants to put the comment down to Miss Bryan's characteristic dottiness. Fortunately under the circumstances, Miss Dundee was only second runner-up. Had she won, I would imagine we would have had girls storming off the stage and yet another "fix" scandal in the press.

I moved into my own flat in West Hampstead, and living two streets away was an actress called Stephanie Beacham. At that time she wasn't a household name and it would be years later before her fame from starring in *Dynasty* and *The Colbys* propelled her onto the judging panels of both Miss Universe 1994 and Miss World 2000.

At Miss World 1975 I would meet two of my all-time favorites - the eventual winner from Puerto Rico, Wilnelia Merced, and Miss Venezuela, Maria Conchita Alonso.

Maria – who was born in Cuba - was an absolute pleasure to be around. I made sure at meal times I was always seated next to her. I had no idea if she had aspirations at that time to be a performer but being in her presence you knew you were with a star in the making and, of course, she went on to an illustrious career in film and show business.

As fabulous as she was, you also knew she was not going to be Miss World (she finished 7th), because from the first time you laid eyes on Wilnelia (Winnie) you were certain that there was no panel of judges who weren't going to recognize what we all did. Wherever you saw her, no matter the setting, you could already see the crown on her head. She was only 18 years old but there had never been a contestant with the poise and regal bearing of this Miss Puerto Rico.

She won easily to no one's surprise (although Eric Morley revealed afterwards that he had only put her 6th) but it was a thrill to watch the reaction backstage of her fellow contestants who jumped for joy and embraced her as she was declared Miss World 1975. They too had known she was deserving and she was just as beautiful inside as she was physically.

On New Year's Day 1976 I flew to Madrid to meet up with Winnie, who was booked to appear on Spain's top rated, late night talk show. While still only a teenager, she was born to be the top international beauty queen - perhaps of all time - as she took her new found role very seriously and intended to leave an indelible imprint as the ultimate Miss World wherever she appeared. On this night she suggested an idea to the show's director so she could make a very dramatic entrance in her beaded gown with a long train by asking him to find a staircase to bring onto the set so she could sweep down rather than just walk on like any other guest.

Anybody who has ever worked in pageants would have been blessed to have had a Winnie to know and accompany on appearances. She became a top model in New York and stayed a good friend. Five years later she was back in London to judge Miss World 1980, alongside boxer Alan Minter, Vice-President of Universal Studios Peter Thompson, actor Dennis Waterman...and one Bruce Forsyth.

At the Miss World office we often debated the sex lives of our titleholders and we all agreed that good Catholic girl Winnie might be our only virgin. One night, a week or so after the Miss World pageant she had judged, we went out to dinner. Afterwards, I presumed I was driving her back to her hotel. But she said she had plans to go and meet a friend and requested being taken to a hotel in South Kensington. I guessed she was going to spend the rest of the evening with a girlfriend. When we got to the hotel, she asked if I would go with her to see her safely to her friend's room. I did so - and imagine my sheer surprise when we knocked on the door and I discovered I had delivered her to Bruce Forsyth! Three years later they were married. After his investiture by the Queen, which took place on 12 October 2011, he became a Sir and the ever lovely Winnie became Lady Forsyth. Sadly, Sir Bruce died in August 2017.

That panel who so rightly chose Winnie as Miss World included two female stars who had an unfortunate encounter of their own at the final. Nyree Dawn Porter and Susan George took the break between the pre-show and the start of the live televised final to locate the nearest ladies' room at the Albert Hall.

Since the panel was situated near a staircase that led to the bowels of the venue - the same area where the dressing rooms for the contestants were located - they descended the stairs and began their search for a bathroom, only to be abruptly stopped by a very stern Miss World security guard who obviously didn't recognize them and who made them feel like terrorists trying to invade the private sanctum of the competitors. Luckily, while they were being dressed down by the security guy, another pageant official wandered by and apologised, in doing so probably preventing the panel having two less celebrities when it went over the airwaves.

Not judging that year was the beloved comedian Ronnie Barker. With less than an hour to go before we had to leave for the Albert Hall for the final, we still had one position left to fill on the panel. Call arounds were being frantically made until the BBC producer's assistant informed us the Beeb had saved the night by getting Mr Barker to agree to judge. Who knows why but Julia, I think, didn't like being told our problem had been solved by the Beeb and made me call back to turn down their offer. I did so and then recommended we should let the last place be taken by the very first Miss World, Kiki Hakansson, who was attending her first Miss World in 24 years. And that is how a former Miss World from Sweden took the spotlight that evening over a British national treasure due to apparently nothing more than plain spite.

My very first task when I joined the Miss World organisation was in locating all past winners and inviting them to come to London for the 25th Anniversary in 1975. Many did return but none of the formers had an easy time getting to London. We did a deal with Sabena Airlines to provide complimentary air fares to the past winners and a guest to accompany them. Great to not have to pay a farthing for their travel - but Sabena had no direct flights in and out of London. All passengers, no matter their point of departure, had to fly into their hub in Brussels to catch another flight to Heathrow. So if you were the 1953 winner Denise Perrier coming from France, you had to fly to London from Paris via Brussels. And she had the least inconvenience. It took many flights and a couple of days for Belinda Green (1972) to make it from Australia or Penny Coelen (1958) from South Africa.

Needless to say, none of them were too happy about the travel arrangements. But Rosemarie Frankland (1961) who arrived with her husband Warren Entner, himself a celebrity musician with the band The Grass Roots, was livid. Not only had they gone halfway around the world just to get from California to London, but Sabena had managed to lose their luggage.

Once at the hotel housing the past winners, Rosemarie called me and expressed her disappointment using very colourful language. I left the official hotel to go to hers bearing peace offerings of flowers and champagne; it didn't appease them. When I asked them what I could do - since I wasn't able to personally retrieve their bags - they told me that the way to calm their nerves after such a traumatic journey was to score some of the middle word of Mr Entner's rock band - and ASAP.

On my walk back to my hotel, I realized their demand wasn't unachievable, since my friend Jimmy knew how to supply us all with high grade marijuana. I called him and impressed upon him the urgency of the situation. Only 15 minutes later, he rang back: sorted. However, he had to go to work and wasn't able to go and collect the goods for me.

I couldn't leave the hotel. Who could I possibly talk into taking a taxi and going to the East End to make a cash transaction to pick up a substance so I could placate Rosemarie and Warren? Who did I settle on to do my dirty work? The most naive young woman from a fine, conservative family who worked for Miss World as a secretary. That's who I sent with instructions to just hand over the envelope I gave her (not letting her know it contained cash) and that she would be given a small package to bring back to me. The time from when she left the hotel in a taxi seemed to crawl by, and I started imagining the absolute worst. Where had I sent this poor child, to what den of iniquity? What if she walked into a set-up and was busted for purchasing illegal drugs? How was I going to explain sending such an innocent on an assignment that would probably lead to her being incarcerated? Just as I was on the verge of a breakdown, she returned and handed over the collection, appearing unfazed by carrying out my instructions.

I wasn't totally relieved as I still had to make the short jaunt to take the concealed package to deliver to Rosemarie and Warren, and on the walk over I kept looking over my shoulder thinking I was going to be the one apprehended. Rosemarie and Warren were suitably impressed that I scored for them, while Sabena delivered their luggage the next day in time for Rosemarie to wear a cocktail dress to a reception instead of the jeans she had arrived in. Little could I have known when presented five years earlier with my first major project what lengths I would have to go to in order to keep harmony at the 25th reunion!

Unwittingly I introduced an inharmonic tone to the event when I suggested to bandleader Phil Tate that I thought the song *It Was A Good Time* would be an ideal opening number to which the past winners would be introduced. Since Ann Sidney, Miss World 1964, had become a professional entertainer the BBC show producer had asked her to perform it, and Phil Tate readily agreed. It was only years later that I listened to the whole original recording by Liza Minelli and became aware that the song, far from being celebratory, was actually about divorce! But, thankfully, Ann's upbeat rendition left out any mention of a bad break-up and came over as the happy song I'd originally intended it to be.

In August 1976 I had the fate of the two biggest beauty queens of that year in my hands. Vying for the Miss United Kingdom title were Carol Grant, Miss Scotland, and Sian Adey-Jones, Miss Wales. Carol had placed fourth in Miss Universe in Hong Kong a month earlier, while Sian came one place higher as second runner-up.

On the day of the Miss UK final at a rehearsal, Julia approached me and wanted to know which of Carol and Sian did I believe would be the better one to win and go forward to Miss World? She explained that the panel of judges - Cliff Michelmore, Shirley-Anne Field, Salena Jones, and Dominic Grant (future son in law of Wilnelia Merced) - were split as to whether the title should go to Carol or Sian. She would relay my decision to Eric who, as chairman, would have the deciding vote. Miss Scotland, my choice, won the title and repeated her Miss Universe placing of 4th at Miss World. Carol later became my "partner in crime" when I left Miss World and "stole" the Miss Universe franchises for England, Ireland, Scotland and Wales from the Morleys.

Making history of a more dubious kind that year was Pauline Davies, who became the first – and only - Miss England in the lifetime of the Miss UK contest to miss out on a place in the Top 15. Having made the semi-final of Miss Universe and been named Miss Photogenic by the world's press whilst out in Hong Kong, Pauline seemed a shoo-in to do well at Miss UK a month later. She was devastated at the news – and the fact that her 'sister' queens Carol Grant and Sian Adey-Jones placed so highly at both pageants left her feeling completely marginalised.

The 1976 Miss World winner was a fitness trainer with Spartan Health Club in Jamaica. Cindy Breakspeare had won the Miss Jamaica Body Beautiful contest, which gave her entry into Miss Universe Bikini final being held in London. She won that international title and her boss, Mickie Houghton-James, sent photos of her to our Miss World office wanting to know if we would accept her as Jamaica's entry into Miss World, despite her not having won a national Miss Jamaica title.

More Misdeameanours tells the full story of how we readily agreed, and how Cindy's 50-1 starting price with Ladbrokes gave me and my colleagues the incentive to do everything we could to ensure her victory. Cindy saw Miss World as an opportunity, saying, "With no family backing and no university education, I made a conscious effort to exploit my God-given talent."

Cindy's win introduced us to a major celebrity - her boyfriend Bob Marley who was eventually the father of their child, reggae artist Damian Robert Nesta "Jr. Gong" Marley. They weren't the first or last to form a beauty queen/celebrity duo, alongside Marji Wallace and Tom Jones, Marji and George Best, Mary Stavin and George Best (he got around), Belinda Green and Rod Stewart, Carolyn Seaward, Miss United Kingdom 1979 and 1st runner-up to Miss World, and Prince Andrew. The latter duo only had one date but it was in Andrew's quarters at Buckingham Palace.

At Miss United Kingdom 1977, the judges were breaking from tradition. Miss England, Miss Scotland and Miss Wales won the right to represent their countries at Miss Universe, as well as automatic entry into Miss United Kingdom to vie for the chance to compete in Miss World. From the time I joined the organisation, I had questioned the fairness of national titleholders - who had experience competing at an international level and, as part of their prize package, received gowns specially designed for them - in competition with those who only bore local titles, many of whom had already been beaten in those national pageants earlier in the year.

The statistics said it all: from 1967-1977, the Miss United Kingdom winners had all been one of the national titleholders, with no less than seven of them being Miss Englands.

I had been assigned the task of sifting through the entries of the photographic heat, the winner of whom would go through to Miss United Kingdom 1977. I was alone in the office when a young lady - who, in her own words, stood at 5'12" - paid me a visit. I knew of Madeleine Stringer from the past year's final when she had made top 7, and today she was asking me to accept her late entry in the photographic heat, having just missed the deadline. Because she had bothered to travel from her home in the north-east all the way to London for this very purpose, I agreed to accept her entry. Not only that, but hers turned out to be the best photo submitted in my opinion, resulting in her winning the heat and being awarded the title of Miss North Shields (her hometown).

I never for one moment thought that my actions would go on to change the established order at Miss United Kingdom, and that someone other than a national titleholder would take the crown!

One month after the photographic heat, Madeleine was in Blackpool for Miss United Kingdom, which was a two-day affair. On day one the contestants paraded in swimsuits, and the judges whittled the field down to 12 or 14 semi-finalists. A place or two in the semi-finals were always left open, to be announced that evening at a formal dinner, during which individual interviews would take place with the judges.

After Madeleine had been announced as a semi-finalist, I travelled with two of the celebrity judges (Paul NIcholas and Coral Atkins) back to our hotel. They were discussing their selections and raving about Madeleine. They felt that she was the British Brooke Shields, then at the height (no pun intended) of her modelling fame in the States with her *"Nothing comes between me and my Calvins"* advert. When I was chatting with a third panelist (the reigning Miss World, Cindy Breakspeare) she too confirmed her choice was Madeleine. Oh my God! It was suddenly very likely that Madeleine might be on the brink of a historical victory, taking the title over one of the national titleholders for the first time in a decade!

During dinner held in a large space at the Locarno Ballroom, I kept staring over at Madeleine at a different table, thinking, if only she knew what could be in store for her the next night. But just as the judges went off into a separate room to start their interviewing of the contestants, the fire alarms suddenly went off. I ran over to a startled Madeleine and grabbed her hand, pulling her behind me to a fire exit, down the steps and out of the building.

Upstairs, the manager of the Locarno announced that the alarm was caused by a small kitchen fire and that there was no need to panic or evacuate. We returned to the dinner, but Madeleine and I never did speak about why I had singled her out as the one contestant I chose to save; she never knew it was because I wanted her to be unharmed to claim her victory the following night live on the BBC.

Looking back, of course, if the three judges planning to give her their first places hadn't been saved from the 'fire' as well, my act of salvage would've been in vain anyway!

But Madeleine did indeed win the crown - a local titleholder was Miss United Kingdom at last, a feat even more remarkable when you consider that the next three winners were national titleholders as well. Madeleine finished sixth at Miss World and after relinquishing her title went on to marry Chas Chandler, the original bassist in The Animals.

A celebrity she and I both encountered when she competed in Miss World was the host of the televised final, American singing star Andy Williams. During her on stage interview as a finalist, Madeleine towered over the diminutive Mr Williams, who was visibly offended when she made reference to the height difference. I offended him by a very different stance I took with him. He was occupying a suite on an upper floor of our official hotel and presumed he could call down to me in the admin office and place his 'order' for any girl he had seen at rehearsals that day to come up and spend time with him. Explaining to his manager that his boss' needs were not going to be satisfied with this kind of arrangement was just another part of the job that had made me immune to seeing or hearing anything that could shock me.

Joining Joan Collins on the 1977 Miss World panel was Oliver Tobias, her co-star in the X-rated film *The Stud*. To get Miss Collins, we had to agree to invite Mr Tobias, a move that pissed off the Morleys and the

Beeb who felt the pageant was being used as a vehicle to promote the soon to be released steamy motion picture. Far less controversial and much better known to worldwide audiences at that time was fellow judge Mickey Dolenz of *The Monkees*.

When I departed Miss World in 1980 and established Amaranth Promotions to select representatives from England, Ireland, Scotland and Wales to go to Miss Universe 1981, we brought the reigning Miss Universe, Shawn Weatherly (ironically from my home state of South Carolina) to London. As part of her itinerary, we took her to the theatre to see a revival of *The Last of Mrs Cheyney* in which Miss Collins was the star. After the performance, we went backstage for an audience with her so that Shawn could hand deliver an invitation to her to join the panel of judges for Miss Universe. Joan was even more beautiful up close. Wearing a short wig for her part in the play, she was standing in front of me and I admit I did inspect her neck for any tell-tale signs of a face lift. Not a scar, not a blemish.

The 1978 Miss World winner came from Argentina and giving her a first place vote was judge Julio Ricardo Villa, a member of the Argentine team who won that year's football World Cup. Silvana Suarez had a rather uneventful reign until her return to crown her successor. Years before Donald Trump belittled his Miss Universe Alicia Machado for gaining too much weight, Julia revealed to the press her concern that Silvana needed to shed some pounds. Perhaps shaming her for changing shape was the catalyst for Silvana to become the first Miss World to appear on the cover of *Playboy* and have a six page pictorial spread.

The honour (?) of being the first *Playboy* model to go full frontal in an edition of the magazine went to another of our beauty queens. Marilyn Cole had been Miss Streatham and a semi-finalist in Miss United Kingdom 1971 while a Playboy Bunny and model. Marilyn was not only the *Playboy* Playmate of the Month in January 1972 and named Playmate of the Year 1973, she married Victor Lownes, Britain's best paid executive as senior VP at Playboy Enterprises. She continued to pose for *Playboy* until 1984 and became a journalist, writing for *The Observer*, *Esquire* and *GQ* magazine.

1979 would turn out to be my last trip to Blackpool for a Miss United Kingdom pageant and the last time I would get into hot water again with the Morleys. The cause for admonishment on this occasion was my booking a celebrity judge without getting their approval first.

During my early days with Mecca Promotions, I worked with a fabulous lady called Anne Miles, who not only obtained sponsorships for all the promotions held in Mecca clubs throughout Britain, but also acted as Press Liaison during Miss World.

Anne left Mecca Promotions and went to work for her husband's record distribution company. We'd kept in touch and she rang me just before the 1979 Miss UK contest to ask if we would consider one of their artistes as a judge? Les McKeown was known for being part of the vastly successful Bay City Rollers, but had just released a solo album (with the title of *All Washed Up* – an in-joke directed at his critics who said his career would be over once he left the band).

I was dubious but, with Julia away for a few weeks, Les agreed to meet me at the office and show how seriously he would take his position on the judging panel. He came in wearing a jump suit unzipped down the front and demonstrating, when he leaned forward showing a flash of his pubes, that he was clearly going commando. An exhibitionist he may have been – as so many rock stars are – but he was also very sweet and humble, and I was so impressed that I rang Anne and booked him as a judge so he could promote his new album.

I got no response, good or bad, from Julia when I told her I'd secured Les as a judge. However, come the final in Blackpool, Les appeared with blue streaks in his hair and, to complement the Asian-influenced phase he was going through, wore a kimono-type outfit for the live show instead of the customary tuxedo. Eric Morley sat uncomfortably beside him and later expressed his displeasure at Les's attire to Julia – who subsequently gave me a reprimand. But I still have the signed copy of the album that Les sent me as a thank you!

Like so many of the celebrity judges during my tenure, Les hit the headlines again 20 years later. At the age of 53, he admitted to having lived a secret gay life for his entire career – one he had kept hidden even from his Japanese wife.

One of the judges at my last Miss World in 1979 was actor Michael Crawford, best known for his antics as Frank Spencer in the TV comedy *Some Mothers Do 'Ave 'Em*, and his theatrical successes starring in *Barnum* and *Phantom of the Opera*.

As was customary in those days, former beauty queens were invited by the Morleys to help the contestants during rehearsals, and that year saw the return of Ann Jones, Miss United Kingdom 1978. In a world exclusive I can reveal that Ann met Michael Crawford at that year's Coronation Ball after the pageant and enjoyed a ten-month romance which has never been revealed to the newspapers. Ann described Michael – who had divorced some years earlier – as "a perfect gentleman" and has only happy memories of one of the last great British performers, who still to this day appears in TV and stage shows.

After leaving the Miss World organisation I did return to Mecca Promotions, but only once Eric Morley had been deposed as Chairman. In the years in between, as well as setting up Amaranth Promotions and staging the *British Festival of Beauty*, I worked with Louis Parker at Concord Management and helped stage the *Malibu World Dance Championships*. In their second year of sponsorship, they made a request: that we secure the services of Bucks Fizz to perform as the headline act at the London final. Louis had a contacts book second to none and Malibu were overjoyed to hear that Bucks Fizz's management had agreed for the group to travel to London after their sold out gig in Newcastle.

But, as happens on so many occasions, God had a custard pie up his sleeve. On the morning of the final – 11th December 1984 – I got into my car to drive to rehearsals and switched the radio on to catch the headline news, only to hear that the tour bus carrying Bucks Fizz and their crew had been involved in a serious collision. Mike Nolan had been rushed to hospital with head injuries and placed on a life support machine, while the other three members had been badly hurt.

Fortunately, all four band members made an eventual recovery, but the terrible events of that day left Malibu without their headline act. Chart-topping singer Billy Ocean agreed to quickly step in at the last minute.

Interestingly, Jay Aston competed in Miss England 1978, where the interval act was that year's Eurovision group, CoCo, featuring one Cheryl Baker. Neither of them could possibly have guessed that night that two years later they would be bandmates in one of the biggest groups of the 80s.

And in 1984 Cheryl Baker was a judge at the Miss World final, alongside Stirling Moss, Mike Read and Mary Stavin.

Due to Mecca's preferred charity being the Variety Club of Great Britain, I got to meet the Queen and Prince Phillip, Prince Charles and Diana, Fergie and many of the lesser Royals like the Duke and Duchess of Kent. I was even awarded Life Patron status with Variety Club and presented with a trophy by Louis Mountbatten, 1st Earl Mountbatten of Burma. The presentation was made on his Shadow V moored on the Thames, the same vessel on which he was assassinated.

Ironically, had my career with Miss World lasted for a few more years, I would have met playboy Dodi Fayed, invited to be a judge at Miss World 1982 as a result of his success as producer of smash-hit movie *Chariots of Fire*. Dodi – whose father owned Harrods - of course died in the tragic car crash in August 1997, which also ended the life of Diana, Princess of Wales.

My favourite celebrity to work with on fundraising events for the Variety Club? 80s pop star Rick Astley. He became the spokesman for the *Kids on The Move With Mecca* campaign, and was such a pleasant personality and hard worker. I am delighted that he made a recent comeback with a No 1 album and is now more popular than ever.

Despite my working with Royalty and the biggest names in sport and show business – from Sasha Distel to Shirley Maclaine, Christine Keeler to Linda McCartney – I was never fazed by celebrity. The only time I have ever been tongue-tied to the point of being unable to converse was when I met someone that most readers will have never heard of!

I had to go up north to judge a heat of Miss United Kingdom and became a blithering idiot when the organiser introduced me to one of my fellow judges: Adele Rose. "WHO?" I hear you say! My all-time favourite TV series is *Coronation Street* – I never missed an episode when I lived in London. And here I was, face to face, with the woman who wrote the majority of the scripts. Forget Prince Charles, forget Joan Collins: I was in celebrity heaven and unable to control my admiration for her!

As I reflect back on the years of celebrity encounters and subsequent exposure to so many scandals, I realise that in the pageant world all publicity is good publicity - at least for Miss World. Would the pageant have been as newsworthy in its heyday if almost every crowning in the 70s hadn't been followed by a front page controversy?

Did the pageant actually court and exploit controversies to ensure it was a topic of water cooler discussions for days after a new Miss World was selected? Most definitely. We may have feigned shock at the high jinks of Marji Wallace, or the out of wedlock baby Helen Morgan revealed a day after becoming Miss United Kingdom. We may have pursed our lips when reading of the relationship between Cindy Breakspeare and a married Bob Morley, or the nude photos of Madeleine Stringer, Silvana Suarez and Gabriella Brum, not forgetting the topless picture of Anneline Kriel leaked to the press. But for all the pretend outrage, these stories sold papers and kept Miss World in the news – which can't be said for the pageant today.

It is the beauty queens whose wins are tainted by controversy that get the most media coverage and are the best remembered. I rest my case.

These days the event doesn't attract celebrities to judge (except maybe ones known only in the host country) or internationally renowned hosts. With the emphasis on the Beauty With A Purpose charity and no swimsuit competition, there seems to be less effort to attract media attention and far less opportunity for a controversy.

Give me the old days back...because who doesn't like a good pageant scandal? Obviously, readers of the *Misdeameanours* series certainly seem to!

Once, Twice, Three Times Miss England

❧ ———————————————————— ❧

"She is wearing a waspie! I demand another contest!"
Mrs Esther Massey, mother of a losing finalist

To paraphrase Lady Bracknell in *The Importance of Being Earnest*, to lose one Miss England may be regarded as a misfortune; to lose two looks like carelessness.

Yet that was the exact scenario facing Eric Morley during scenes worthy of an Oscar Wilde comedy following the 1958 Miss England contest, when three winners were crowned in the space of three weeks.

The furore started when miner's daughter June Cooper was crowned the winner in the final shown live on BBC television. The beguiling green-eyed beauty from Sheffield had worked in a shop since leaving school, and had turned up to the Miss England contest with a second-hand dress and borrowed swimsuit, so sure was she that she wouldn't win.

But win she did. Yet only five days later, June's new crown was returned to the organisers. Shortly after her victory it was discovered that she was 27 days under the minimum permitted age limit of 17, despite her having signed a declaration before the contest stating that she was within the rules.

A meeting between the organisers and June's mother was hurriedly arranged, and it was announced that she had resigned as Miss England. "The reason for the withdrawal is a simple one," the statement said. "Mrs Cooper, having seen the itinerary which her daughter would follow and the events, such as cocktail parties, which she would have to attend, decided she was too young."

June therefore forfeited a trip to Turkey to compete in Miss Europe, and another to the States for the Miss Universe pageant. She was, however, given £100 in cash as a consolation prize.

"I'm relieved at not having to face the ordeal of going to Turkey and America," she said, before returning home to Sheffield.

With the Miss England throne now unexpectedly vacant again, Eric Morley scheduled a second contest to take place within the fortnight.

The new pageant was held at London's Café de Paris and when the crown went to 22-year-old model Wendy Peters, Mr Morley could have been forgiven for breathing a sigh of relief.

But his satisfaction was short-lived. The crown had barely been laid on Wendy's brunette locks when onto the stage stormed a woman from the audience, believed to be Esther Massey, the mother of a losing finalist, who pushed aside host Wally Green and proceeded to angrily accuse the beauty queen of wearing a waspie – a type of corset - beneath her bathing suit, and that she had therefore cheated. "I demand another contest!" Mrs Massey shouted as she was hustled from the stage.

Another finalist, Barbara Smith, burst into tears. "It's not fair," she sobbed, "I feel we've been cheated."

Wendy was adamant that she hadn't broken the rules. "A waspie is not an artificial aid," she protested. "I merely wear it to stop my bathing costume from rippling."

In years to come, Mecca would state in their rules that all 'artificial aids', including tights, body stockings, corsets and padding, were banned and that any evidence of such would lead to disqualification. Indeed, assistants would be employed to carry out hands-on checks of the girls' clothing to make sure nobody was flouting the rules.

But back in 1958, with the Miss England pageant still very much in its infancy, Eric Morley took a more relaxed view of proceedings and refused to take the crown from his new winner. "So many of the girls were wearing bones and corsets that we decided that unless they had false busts we would turn a blind eye," he said.

Of the objections after the contest, he added: "I can understand the girls getting a bit hysterical," he added, "but not the mothers."

"The fuss took all the joy out of winning," wept Wendy Peters. "I look just as slim without the waspie anyway."

While artificial aids were able to slip through the net on this occasion, it was undisputedly against the Miss England rules to be married. And Wendy Peters was about to drop a second bombshell that would end the shortest of reigns in a way that Corset-gate couldn't.

In a bid to show the world that Wendy didn't need a waspie to be a winner, a photoshoot had been arranged in which she would pose in a bikini to prove her natural credentials. When she didn't show up, the official excuse was that she was ill.

But neighbours at her £3,000 three-bedroom home in Byfleet were able to shed some light on what had really happened. They knew her not as Wendy Peters, but Wendy Maitland, wife of David, a former Lieutenant Commander in the Royal Navy.

Eric Morley confirmed that his second Miss England in the space of two weeks had entered the contest under false pretences. "I discovered today that Wendy was married when I examined her passport and other papers," he said. "She said that she had been separated from her husband for two and a half years, and in her mind this was as good as not being married.

"I am going to have to decide if she should be disqualified. If she's not eligible we will have to hold the contest all over again.

In the end, Wendy made the decision for him, and resigned her title. She told the *Daily Mirror*, "I'm afraid I told a great big white lie when I filled in the application form. But I never dreamed for a moment that I would win."

When asked if she was upset about giving up the title, Wendy was adamant that she wasn't. "At present I'm earning about £50 a week modelling," she said, "so why should I worry about competitions?"

An exasperated Morley announced, with understandable weariness, that the girls who had taken part in the second contest would all compete again in the third the following week. But this time there were two strict rules in place: that each girl must bring along her passport to prove her age and marital status, and that there must be nothing between herself and her swimsuit.

At last it was third time lucky, when a 19-year-old blonde called Dorothy Hazeldine became Miss England 1958 Mk 3, having finished fourth and second respectively in the past two aborted contests. The beauty parlour assistant from Rochdale was, happily, found to be both unmarried and unpadded.

Dorothy went on to represent England in both Miss Europe and Miss Universe, but didn't place in either pageant.

David Maitland, husband of the second winner Wendy Peters, was granted a divorce from his wife in 1961, on the grounds of her desertion five years earlier.

But the real star of that tumultuous year was the original winner, June Cooper. She bounced back just three months after resigning her Miss England crown to win the national title of Ideal Holiday Girl 1958, beating 15 other finalists to the prize of £250 and entry to the Miss United Kingdom pageant.

June, who was 17 by then, told the press that she had left her shop assistant job. "In two weeks' time I start as a dress model in London's West End."

She proved to be an extremely popular and successful model, and soon landed the role as hostess on the ITV quiz show *Double Your Money*, alongside legendary host Hughie Green. A career as an actress beckoned and June appeared in the 1964 James Bond movie

Goldfinger, and the MGM classic *Yellow Rolls Royce*, as well as roles in several of the films in the *Carry On* franchise.

June married factory manager David Purkiss in 1962 and they moved to Essex where they had a daughter, Nicola, who followed in mum's footsteps and also became a model.

As for the Miss England pageant, it would be 51 years before another winner would have to relinquish her crown. Rachel Christie resigned after a fight with another beauty queen in a nightclub in 2009, a story covered in full In *Misdemeanours* Vol 1.

Mis-3-meanours can exclusively reveal a fascinating footnote concerning the third and final Miss England 1958, Dorothy Hazeldine, when she returned to the pageant scene 13 years later.

Dorothy won the Million Dollar Legs title at London's Lyceum Theatre in 1971, a prestigious nationwide contest sponsored by Woolworths. However it was discovered that the beauty queen – competing under her married name of Dorothy Whitehead – had lied about her age. Dorothy was, at 33, over the maximum age limit by three years, having declared on her entry form that she was 25.

Just like her 1958 counterpart, she was stripped of her title and ordered to return her £500 prize money.

Yet the connection between Dorothy Whitehead and Dorothy Hazeldine has only been revealed now, nearly 50 years later, in *Mis-3-meanours*. It didn't occur to organisers Mecca – nor to the press - that the lady who had fibbed about her age was the same beauty who had taken over their 1958 Miss England title after the original winner had told the exact same porkie all those years before.

Also by the same author: